"We go down too many rabbit holes when discussing assessment, tests, data, and evidence. Angela Stockman provides a powerful perspective focusing on interpreting the myriad of information that teachers, leaders and students encounter in every lesson. The book introduces the concept of *documentation*, which involves investigating the people, places, processes, practices, and products of teaching and learning. Through this approach, educators are encouraged to triangulate, deduce, induce, and find meaning, ultimately taking purposeful actions in their teaching journey. This book serves as a valuable gift, empowering teachers with a fresh perspective and the ability to make a significant impact on their students' learning experiences."

**Professor John Hattie,** *University of Melbourne Australia.*
*A global authority on education effectiveness, his extensive research is the world's largest evidence base on what works best in schools to improve learning.*

"As we inch towards the overdue transformation of education into a learning ecosystem that places learning, and learners, at the heart of our work, key necessities rise to the surface. One of these is the need to shift away from assessment as *accounting*, with its focus on low-level, high-stakes, quantitative grading, and towards assessing what actually *counts*. This means learning how to look for, and document, a range of valid evidence of student learning, owned and curated by learners themselves. This profound move towards assessing what we truly value places documentation at the heart of our work as learning professionals. In this wonderful book, Angela confirms the central place of the documentation of learning, both our students' and our own. She does so with the clarity and confidence of a seasoned and reflective practitioner and in a voice that feels like your favourite colleague in the next classroom. I loved this important and engaging book, and will keep it close, as a key ally in the struggle towards authentic, evidence-based learning."

**Kevin Bartlett,** *initiator and early leader of the International Baccalaureate Primary Years Program, Founding Director of the Common Ground Collaborative, and former Director of the International School of Brussels (ISB).*

T0373579

# The Writing Teacher's Guide to Pedagogical Documentation

This book is a call to action for English and English Language Arts teachers who understand that data are not numbers alone, learning is impossible to quantify, and students are our very best teachers.

Writing teacher Angela Stockman shows us how pedagogical documentation—the practice of making learning visible, capturing what is seen and heard, and then interpreting those findings in the company of our students and our colleagues—is a humbling and humane practice that grounds what we think we've come to know in the lived experiences of those we intend to serve. In this rich resource, she offers:

◆ processes and protocols for documenting learning and analyzing data;
◆ resources and planning tools to help you design and execute your own projects; and
◆ a digital documentation notebook that you can download for guidance, inspiration, and examples.

With the powerful tools in this book, you'll be inspired to reach students whose needs have been ignored by big data and whose identities have been erased by oppressive forms of assessment and evaluation.

**Angela Stockman** spent 12 years teaching at the elementary, middle, and high school levels before becoming a professional learning facilitator. Currently, she continues to support thousands of literacy teachers in K-12 schools throughout the United States and Canada. In her role as the Executive Director of Distance Education at Daemen University, she also enjoys working beside higher education faculty and staff to create and facilitate quality learning experiencesfor undergraduate and graduate students alike. She continues to teach and document her learning there.

## Also Available from Angela Stockman
(www.routledge.com/K-12)

Inclusive Writing Environments in the K-12 Classroom: Reluctance, Resistance, and Strategies that Make a Difference

The Writing Workshop Teacher's Guide to Multimodal Composition (K-5)

The Writing Workshop Teacher's Guide to Multimodal Composition (6-12)

# Online Tools

This book is accompanied by online tools to help you on your pedagogical documentation journey.

- **Digital documentation notebook:** This living document offers clear examples of the approaches to pedagogical documentation described in the book, as well as case studies contributions from other documentarians. You can access it on the author's website (https://angelastockman.com/blog/2023/08/02/my-digital-documentation-notebook/) using the password Documentarian.
- **Pedagogical Documentation Needs Assessment:** An online survey (https://bit.ly/45UCzxz)
- **Downloads:** The tools in Part III are also available on the Routledge website as free downloads. To access them, go to Routledge.com/9781032366319 and click on the link that says Support Material.

# The Writing Teacher's Guide to Pedagogical Documentation

Rethinking How We Assess Learners and Learning

Angela Stockman

Routledge
Taylor & Francis Group

NEW YORK AND LONDON

Designed cover image: © Shutterstock

First published 2024
by Routledge
605 Third Avenue, New York, NY 10158

and by Routledge
4 Park Square, Milton Park, Abingdon, Oxon, OX14 4RN

*Routledge is an imprint of the Taylor & Francis Group, an informa business*

*Library of Congress Cataloging-in-Publication Data*
Names: Stockman, Angela, author.
Title: The writing teacher's guide to pedagogical documentation : rethinking how we assess learners and learning / Angela Stockman.
Description: New York, NY : Routledge, 2024. | Includes bibliographical references and index. |
Identifiers: LCCN 2023043988 (print) | LCCN 2023043989 (ebook) | ISBN 9781032366814 (hardback) | ISBN 9781032366319 (paperback) | ISBN 9781003333241 (ebook)
Subjects: LCSH: Composition (Language arts)--Study and teaching--Evaluation. | English language--Composition and exercises--Study and teaching--Evaluation.
Classification: LCC PN181 .S75 2024 (print) | LCC PN181 (ebook) | DDC 372.62/3044--dc23/eng/20231031
LC record available at https://lccn.loc.gov/2023043988
LC ebook record available at https://lccn.loc.gov/2023043989

ISBN: 978-1-032-36681-4 (hbk)
ISBN: 978-1-032-36631-9 (pbk)
ISBN: 978-1-003-33324-1 (ebk)

DOI: 10.4324/9781003333241

Typeset in Palatino
by KnowledgeWorks Global Ltd.

Access the Support Material: www.routledge.com/9781032366319

# Contents

# Acknowledgments

Too often, it's only the authors of the books who get the applause.

But ten years ago, while I was off designing units and lessons and documentation plans, my husband was painting the walls of the WNY Young Writers' Studio, building our furniture, and overseeing the installation of plumbing and sinks so we could paint stories together.

While I was making tinker totes, he was building shelves in our garage to house my many bins of loose parts and two decades' worth of documentation notebooks. He lifted those bins from shelf to trunk each time I was invited to create pop-up studios in spaces that weren't my own. And he kept the home fires burning while I was away.

While I was coding my data all over our living room floor, my husband was pouring me countless cups of coffee and pointing out features I'd missed. He was cooking all of our meals, cleaning our house, doing our laundry, packing my lunch, and firing up the heating pad every time my body began breaking under the weight of seven books, and all of the words that cost me time with him. He put eyes on every draft as it took shape, offered critical feedback that those who are far too close to education could never provide, and never complained about the pile of books and index cards that consumed our kitchen table for over a year.

He did this while transitioning into a new career of his own, helping our adult daughters move into and out of many apartments, raising a pandemic puppy into a 140-pound bundle of joy, and supervising the reconstruction of our basement, garage, and entire kitchen.

This book—and nearly every good thing about my life—exists because of John Stockman.

So, please clap for him a bit and for every partner who helps those they love bring books into the world.

Because we don't do that enough.

# Introduction

I remember the day when Max brought their LEGOs into our writing studio. I remember how the teachers nudged me toward their table.

"Look at what they're doing," one said. "Listen."

And of course I did.

Max was building a story, one brick at a time. As they tinkered with their build, their narrative unfolded, shape-shifted, and settled into a familiar sort of something. It was fascinating—watching their hands steady the composition. They were focused and decisive. They were purposeful in their play.

They weren't the child I'd met the day before.

Max didn't produce written words then, but there was something in the way that they were working with their LEGOs that demonstrated their mastery of the narrative form I'd been trying to nudge out of them all week. When they started bantering about their build, their story captured our teacher's hearts. They weren't speaking to us, of course. They were role-playing inside the imaginary world that set the scene for a story that seemed far more complex than any other writer's story in the room.

I remember holding my breath, my face burning with the realization that I'd had them all wrong. Max wasn't a struggling writer. The struggle had been my own. This realization changed everything—my practice, the way that Max and I engaged with one another, and the way that I would continue to learn about teaching writing well for decades to come.

Max appeared in my very first book—*Make Writing*—published in 2015. Those first moments of discovery were also the very beginning of a learning

DOI: 10.4324/9781003333241-1

journey that I'm still navigating my way through. As I learn more about what it means to serve different kinds of learners, documentation has been an essential companion inside of a field that is still in its infancy and enduring its own growing pains. It consistently lifts me above the fray and points me toward productive next steps.

If you'd have asked me in the moment, I'd have said that Max was a game-changer. I wouldn't have noticed this if I wasn't documenting my learning, though. While experts have much to share and theories about what constitutes a best practice continue to form and then crumble inside of current realities, I know that this much is true: Developing the dispositions of documentation has made me a far better teacher. It illuminated pathways through deep darkness and quieted the noise that always echoes in such spaces. It helped me move writers forward. That isn't why I want you to read this book, though. I want you to read this book because documentation has made the whole of my life deeply worthwhile in ways it wouldn't be otherwise. It's also kept me hungry, happy, and able to be awestruck at any given moment. Documentation is about living my life in full color as well rather than suffering a sepia-toned existence. This is what I want for you.

## What Is Documentation?

As I write this introduction to my seventh book, seven years after I introduced Max in my first, I realize it wasn't simply the learning or the fact that it was documented that made my experience with that particular young writer so meaningful. It was how documentation changed the story Max was telling themselves about their learning. It was how it widened our aperture as teachers, too. All of us noticed things that typically remain obscured, and while many of them weren't captured in our photos, videos, or annotations, the dedicated act of gathering these artifacts with intention—even as beginners—created a sort of backchannel in our brains and a spirited connection between us where discoveries were made before, during, and after those recorded moments. It was a kind of kindling. It remains so, for me.

Documenting learning was nurturing for all of us. We became more perceptive and patient, approaching each opportunity with a sort of child-like wonder that fed our shared fascinations. This resonance humbled me as a teacher, connected all of us to our most creative and thoughtful selves, and deepened our respect for one another.

The practice of documentation challenges us to make learning visible, listen, observe, and then capture what we notice by making notes, gathering artifacts, taking pictures, or making audio or video recordings. Over time, these habits help us move beyond simple practice. They help us *become* documentarians—teachers who bear close witness to students' lived learning experiences and then use what they discover to create and share theories that serve themselves and others well.

Documentation changes how we think about, interpret, and evaluate what we see and hear in learning spaces. Dr. John Hattie, Professor of Education and Director of the Visible Learning Labs from the University of Auckland, New Zealand, emphasizes the importance of this shift in his revolutionary text, *Visible Learning: The Sequel, A Synthesis of Over 2100 Meta-Analyses Relating to Achievement* (2023). A prominent researcher in the field who is read and highly regarded worldwide, Hattie emphasizes the impact of studying our learning on our abilities to teach. He contends that student achievement has less to do with teacher subject matter knowledge than the willingness of teachers to position themselves as learners who make a dedicated study of the processes that students use and their influence on learning outcomes. He speaks to the steady presence of passion inside of his research findings, its influence on achievement outcomes, and the difference it makes for teachers and learners alike (Hattie, 2023, pp. 7–8).

While many books have been written about the process and craft of writing, instructional practices for those who intend to teach both, and the way educators might best approach curriculum and assessment design, there aren't enough that describe how educators at every level of instruction might become more passionate practitioners by inviting pedagogical documentation to change the way they think about, interpret, and assess learners and learning. That is what this book aims to do.

I hope that reading it inspires and equips you to document your own learning in ways that rejuvenate and sustain you. I hope it helps you recognize your students as your very best teachers and regard their documentation of their own learning as essential evidence. Becoming a documentarian is a metamorphosis like no other. Once transformed, you'll find your vision sharper, your thinking a bit slower, and your heart easily humbled by even the smallest revelations.

Documentarians possess distinct dispositions, and cultures of documentation are unmistakable. They are learning communities dedicated to deepening empathy, awareness, and understanding. They're learner rather than teacher-centered. They embrace uncertainty, lean into discomfort, treat research as a daily discipline, and share what they discover generously. Documentarians try to notice what others might miss, and they tap shoulders, turning people's attention toward what they've made visible. Documentation is all about discovery, and what we discover is often unexpected.

Like many, my early work with documentation was all about aligning my purposes with my practices and tools. I began by establishing some simple habits of documentation and tinkering with different approaches. There were many false starts, and this is when I learned how to share my work with others in order to gain different perspectives. This has continued to benefit me in many other contexts over time, even as I've sharpened and varied my practices and tools.

Facts and truth are very different things, and documentation is about telling the truth as we see it. This is a beautiful thing that can also be highly problematic. This is why it's so essential to co-construct meaning with those who will be most affected by our work and then seek insights beyond our small communities. As teachers, we might be learning about them, but that learning needs to be led by them and our interpretations need to be interrogated if we're to have any hope of overcoming our own inherent biases. If we can accomplish this, we might also realize the opportunity to leverage documentation in service to far greater purposes that extend well beyond the four walls of any classroom. In my opinion, this is its greatest potential. Documentation has the unique power to inspire direct action in a way that other kinds of inquiry and other forms of assessment may not. As a storymaker, I'm also drawn to its narrative nature. I'm pulled in by each plot that seems to unfold around characters who are made more multifaceted by each conflict they confront and the settings they learn within.

## Documentation as Authentic Assessment

The stories that documentarians create are richly textured. They're made of images and artifacts, light and shadow, gesture and sound. Multimedia tools help us share the whole of them. Through the combined use of photographs, audio recordings, sketches, notes, and videos, learners are able to capture and share compelling portraits of their own learning that quickly engage others. They also appear far more complete than those that the adults in their lives typically keep about them—often tidy conclusions that live on clipboards or inside of gradebooks. They're the kinds of data that punctuate progress reports, spreadsheets, and report cards. Often composed with sturdy little letters or cool percentages, they help professionals feel more confident about the theories we're creating. It's easy to think we know something—or someone—when we're working with very limited and quantitative data. Too easy.

Can learning ever be quantified? My friend Jennifer Borgioli Binis put this question in front of me long ago. And what are the unintended consequences of trying? I continue to wonder today. These data are often hard and cold and shallow. They're gathered fast, tethered to narrow outcomes or standards, and then presented to school and community leaders in ways that allow for efficient meaning-making.

And so much is lost along the way.

Documentation challenges us to slow down and steady our gaze—to notice and to pay attention, and then share our discoveries with others. It calls us to question more than we conclude and to continue striving to make the stories we tell about learners and our own learning increasingly whole. This is authentic assessment and instruction. It has the power to shift our purposes, our energy, and our commitment to our work. This may be what makes it so uncomfortable for those who seek silver bullets, fast answers, and especially—power.

Here's something else: Teaching can be isolating and even alienating work. Classrooms are often very lonely places. Documentation changes this. And that change may happen in the moment or in the days and weeks that follow an event or even—as their current writing process is teaching me—decades later when we revisit what we took the time to capture and share so long ago. More than a muse—documentation is a critical friend who reminds us to slow down, take a beat, notice what matters, and what we might otherwise miss. Documentation is a candid co-teacher who never retires until we invite them to.

## Deepening Our Relationship with Documentation

Like all authentic relationships, the one we maintain with documentation is typically imperfect and complex—especially if it stands the test of time. And like all authentic relationships, documentation often holds a mirror to our faces—inviting us to see ourselves in ways that are as clarifying as they are confusing; as affirming as they are unsettling. While many promote documentation as a practice that makes us better assessors or diagnosticians, experience has taught me that unless we are willing to be changed by the process, the conclusions that we draw from our documentation may do great harm. This requires us to recognize and take responsibility for the perspectives and privileges we bring to the work. We have a responsibility here. Documentation isn't about illuminating deficits in order to somehow repair children. It's about developing our humanity and using it in service to others. Documentation elevates awareness, reveals intersectionalities, and complicates our thinking and our feelings—if we allow this, and we must if we're to practice it well.

Readers who come to this text seeking protocols and tools that will enable them to make their learning visible and then capture it well will likely be satisfied by what they find here. Those who are eager to learn more about how learners and learning are changed by documentation will find good guidance as well. Can documentation improve learning outcomes and student performance? It has, in my experience, and I've shared those stories with some of you in the past. My previous books revealed what I learned from documentation. In them, I offered you my conclusions. I shared new and promising instructional practices, and I showed up to test them beside you in some of your classrooms and across the distance, too.

And that was necessary work, but I'm realizing that this was not enough.

In fact, Hattie might suggest that I've spent far too much time telling you what I've done and far too little explaining how I went about doing it (Hattie, 2023, p. 46). I haven't shared how I documented my own learning, let alone invited you to do the same. What's worse: I haven't offered you the tools you might need to become a student of your own teaching, so that you might be transformed by your own discoveries rather than indiscriminately lifting and dropping the theories I've shared into your own instructional plans.

My greater purpose for writing this book is even greater than all of these things, though.

Learning matters, and while documentation allows you to capture, study, and share it, I hope that this text will prepare you to do much more. I hope that it serves as a map and a guide for those of you who are ready to live your lives in full color. I hope it offers the tools that will change your purposes, your practices, and your energy, too. I hope it lifts you above the monotony of monochrome meaning-making and welcomes you into a vibrant world where the stories we make about what happens in our small classrooms improve teaching and learning and yes, our entire lives and those of others as well. You'll find me and so many others there, above the fray, waiting for you.

If you're about to close the cover because this feels like a bunch of self-interested navel-gazing, then this is actually the perfect book for you. Perhaps it's time to clarify your own intentions, quiet the noise, and connect to a deeper something in yourself and in your students, too. Documentation is a coefficient process. It's synergetic. Harmonizing. Documentarians will tell you that the practice enables them to check multiple boxes on their great big to-do lists all at once. It helps them see important relationships, patterns, and trends in their doing, too. I hope that documentation can eventually accomplish the same for you.

## How This Book Is Organized

The first part of this book offers a clear definition of pedagogical documentation, its purposes, and essential practices. Here, you will learn how to use this book, over and over again, to document for different purposes, depending on your shifting interests and needs. You'll explore some tools that will help you define both before choosing the right pathway for any new project. You'll be invited to craft your own documentarian projects—big or small. To that end, you might find yourself lingering over some parts of this book for a long while, digging deeply into others, and ignoring sections that aren't yet relevant to you. You might find a resource in the appendix that captures far more of your attention than the stories I'm offering you. You might find one tool that matters more than this entire collection of chapters. I hope that each time you revisit this book in the future, it feels entirely new to you. I hope you use it to chase different purposes. You may turn different pages along the way, then. I want this book to remain an essential companion as you become a seasoned documentarian, a teacher who is better able to interpret learning experiences through their students' eyes and, as Hattie impels us, strives to know their impact (Hattie, 2023, p. 56).

The second part of this book introduces processes, protocols, and practices that will help you make your learning visible, document it well, find critical friends, analyze the data you gather, and share what you learn. Here you will encounter a wide variety of differentiated prompts and project ideas, case and use studies, and planning frameworks that will guide your initial attempts to document small moments and the sustained journeys and expeditions that will hopefully follow.

I've left a TLDR (too long, didn't read) section at the end of each chapter included in Parts I and II for those of you who need succinct summaries. You'll find invitations to reflect and to try specific tools and approaches there as well. If you haven't accessed the supplemental digital documentation notebook that accompanies their text, you'll want to be sure to do that too, before you begin reading in earnest. This is where I plan to share peeks into my own documentation work, besides reflections and insights from other documentarians in the field. A few of them are colleagues whose sustained experiences with documentation have been especially illuminating. I introduce them in the first chapter and weave their stories and reflections throughout the entire text. They offer insights that I alone cannot, and I hope you find them as compelling as I do. You may follow the threads of their stories as I weave them through the book by looking for their friendly faces, positioned near their biographies in this introductory chapter.

*Kenisha Bynoe co-authored* The Gift of Playful Learning: A Guide for Educators *(Shell Education, 2023) beside Angelique Thompson, mentioned below. An early reading coach for the Toronto District School Board, Kenisha teaches me much about what it means to document learning rather than the mere products of it.*

*Lisa Green is a second-grade teacher in West Valley Central School District just outside of Buffalo, New York. The most passionate documentarian I've had the pleasure of learning beside, Lisa's practice has evolved in recent years, and her commitment to this work has helped her become a more reflective and joyful practitioner.*

*Silence Karl is a sixteen-year-old documentarian from Cattaraugus-Allegany County, New York. His perspectives as a self-directed, homeschooled learner, storymaker, and videographer revealed much to me about how stories are found, captured, and shared.*

*Klara Redford is an early years educator and a teacher-librarian who serves a very diverse group of K-8 students in Thornwood Public School, Mississauga, Ontario. Her experiences inviting loose parts to play inside of literacy spaces have taught me much about the relationship between making and writing over the years.*

*Aaron Schorn is an educator and entrepreneur who co-designs learning programs centered in youth agency, authenticity, and storytelling. The Head of Growth and Community at Unrulr, he's helped me create a documentation culture inside the classes I teach at Daemen University.*

*Angelique Thompson is an early reading coach for the Toronto District School Board, an Additional Qualifications instructor, a French immersion educator, and the co-author of The Gift of Playful Learning (Shell Education, 2023). She works beside Kenisha Bynoe, and her professional generosity has helped me see into and better understand her incredible work.*

The third part of this book includes resources and planning tools that will help you shift from reading in order to gain a surface understanding of pedagogical documentation to designing and executing your own projects. This is where you'll put the knowledge gained in Parts I and II to good use. To that end, you will be invited to interact and if you choose—download a planner that will help you design and work through your own documentation project. My digital documentation notebook, a multimedia companion to this text, will offer additional guidance, inspiration, and examples that might inspire your own work, too.

My digital documentation notebook is a companion text that includes peeks into my own documentation work. There, you will explore moments, journeys, and entire expeditions where I've put the ideas I share in this book to use in my own classroom and studio as well as the schools that I am fortunate to work in. Other colleagues in the field are featured there, too. You may access it through the appendix.

## Who Should Read This Book?

This book is written for K-12 literacy teachers and higher education instructors who are ready to move beyond antiquated assessment practices in order to begin curating and sharing whole stories about teaching and learning. It can be read cover-to-cover but it doesn't have to be. This is a text that can be returned to over time and a tool whose utility will grow as you and the learners you serve deepen your understanding of documentation and tinker and play with these tools and practices in your own learning communities.

# Who Am I?

I began my career as an elementary teacher, spent some time teaching high school English, and then settled into a long stretch as a middle school English Language Arts instructor. In that capacity, I was fortunate to be asked to design and then teach within a dedicated writing workshop program that sat adjacent to students' English Language Arts class. The opportunity to have this kind of daily time with young writers was rare then, and I know that it's even rarer now. I learned much from that magical, messy, and imperfect experience, which left good stones in my shoes.

They were still cutting into my heels when I was invited to serve as a regional literacy specialist for Erie County in western New York State in 2004. Here, I worked within our 26 component school districts and their varied buildings designing curricula and assessments and facilitating professional learning about best practices for writing instruction. The lessons learned from that experience inspired me to establish a lasting learning community for young writers and writing teachers in 2008. Here, I began doing dedicated action research in the company of kids and teachers who knew that all of us had much to learn about what writing was and how to serve young writers well.

This little Studio, close to my home, is where I get to tinker and play with documentation before bringing the best of my learning into the systems

I serve. It's where some of the teachers inside of those systems are able to step out of them for a moment and come and study writers in the wild. Exciting action research projects begin here and are often carried back into our classrooms. Lasting professional friendships are formed, too. We will celebrate our fifteenth year together in 2023.

I am also a full-time Instructional Designer for Daemen University in Amherst, New York, where I teach in the education department. I've recently begun documenting my learning inside of each of these new roles, and I coach my students to do the same as each semester unfolds. Some of our stories will be shared in the chapters that follow.

Finally, a portion of each month finds me in K-12 writing classrooms, facilitating lesson studies, or testing newly designed curricula with the teachers who collaboratively constructed it. If you've read any of my previous books, then you know that their work is dedicated to bringing multimodal expression and composition into our English or English Language Arts classrooms and developing the curriculum, instructional strategies, and assessment and reporting methods that help learners thrive in such spaces.

Those who've tasked me with improving assessment performance in the past have often been surprised by the ways in which I engage teachers and learners in that effort. Time and again, performance improves when we hone our abilities to inquire, theorize, and align our teaching with the discoveries we make about learners and learning while remaining committed to a vision that honors and elevates voice, choice, and creative expression. We improve performance by documenting learning. This isn't documentation's greatest purpose, though. In fact, I hope that one day, Americans in particular will live in a culture where evaluation and testing are valued far less. In the meantime, I'll continue to bring better tools to the work of improving learning outcomes for children, because in the absence of them over-testing will continue to do great harm to learners and teachers alike. Documentation humbles and humanizes us. It helps us seek and share better stories about learners and learning and what it means to teach in their dynamic and multi-colored world.

In recent years, I've been further inspired by the work of scholars Shane Safir and Jamila Duncan. Their book, *Street Data: A Next Generation Model for Equity, Pedagogy, and School Transformation* (Shane & Jamila, 2021) is one that I often recommend to my students and faculty members alike, and while this book does not directly reference theirs, I would be remiss to not mention it here and acknowledge the incredible contribution these educators continue to make to my own scholarship. Likewise, Sarah Zerwin, the author of *Pointless: An English Teacher's Guide to More Meaningful Grading* (Zerwin, 2020), deserves my acknowledgment and sincere gratitude here as well. These are visionary leaders whose dedication to criticality and courageous practice helps all of us do better. I hope that what I share honors the spirit and intention behind their work.

## Some Thoughts About Mitigating Bias

Those who commit to pedagogical documentation know that it's impossible to serve anyone well without deepening our self-awareness, examining the influence of our identities on our practices, gathering critical friends, and interrogating the biases that are inherent in all of our work. We do harm when we allow the assumptions we make about learners and learning to go unchecked.

This text offers consistent reminders and recommendations that will help you mitigate bias in your own work, and Chapters 7 and 8 in particular make a much deeper study of specific approaches. Before you begin, understand that there is no list of items for you to efficiently tick-off in your efforts to do right by others, though. There are only opportunities to deepen your awareness of where you come from and where you don't, what you've experienced and what you have not, and who you are and who you are not. Positionality matters, and so does humility. In the chapters that follow, we'll explore strategies for co-creating documentation projects with your students, relying on multiple measures of assessment, seeking diverse perspectives, and taking care to frame and share your theories responsibly or possibly not at all if they have the potential to do harm.

We don't know what we don't know though, do we? This is why critical friends are essential companions and our dedication to whole-hearted and culturally sustaining practices must be unwavering. I hope I model this well, but know that I am still a beginner. I have much to learn from others, including, perhaps, many of you.

## Honoring the Identities of the Learners I Serve

If you've been following my work for a while, you may already notice that I'm revisiting anecdotes from my previous books in this new one. As you might imagine, the children who taught me much once-upon-a-time are now teenagers and adults, and all of them are very different people. In some cases, they've stopped going by their childhood nicknames. In others, they've realized that their gender isn't what their parents thought it was, and they move through the world differently now. In order to honor all of the changes life has brought them, I've begun using their preferred names and pronouns when revisiting the stories I've told before. I'm grateful to my dear friend Jennifer Borgioli Binis for helping me find the right words and approach here. This is an important practice, and she remains one of my best personal and critical friends.

## References

Bynoe, K., & Thompson, A. (2023). *The gift of playful learning: A guide for educators*. Shell Education.

Hattie, J. (2023). *Visible learning: The sequel*. Taylor Francis Ltd. https://doi.org/10.4324/9781003380542

Shane, S., & Jamila, D. (2021). *Street data: A next-generation model for equity, pedagogy, and school transformation*. Sage Publications, Inc.

Stockman, A. (2015). *Make writing: 5 strategies that turn writer's workshop into a makerspace*. Times Ten Publications.

Zerwin, S. M. (2020). *Point-less: An English teacher's guide to more meaningful grading*. Heinemann.

# Part I

# An Introduction to Documentation

# 1

# What Is Documentation?

I was forever changed the moment Max picked up their LEGOs and began building their story. It wasn't what they were doing or how they were doing it that made such a lasting impression on my practice, though. It was the fact that we took care to observe, document, and make thoughtful interpretations of that moment and so many other connected moments that followed it.

As you might recall from the introduction, when Max began to play, another teacher in the room called me over. "Look," she said, gesturing toward the build. "Listen." I don't have a photo or a video recording of this moment. I have loosely scribbled annotations that I placed inside of the notebook I was carrying that day. They live beside a photo that Max sent me after they'd returned home later that afternoon when something really interesting happened. They'd begun using LEGOs to build a paragraph, and they wanted me to see what they'd made. So, they asked their mom to text a photo. We took many more of those in the months that followed, following Max's journey from the moment they crossed the threshold of our little writing studio to the day they stood at the front of it, leading a brief workshop for other teachers who were eager to learn from them. We weren't clear about our purposes as documentarians then. We were beginners, but as I write this chapter so many years later, I find myself wondering: Was Max's story so influential because they approached the writing process in an uncommon way, or was it influential because we documented it with such enthusiastic intention and then shared it with others in order to gain their perspectives? Was it what Max did as a writer or what it taught so many of us about how we might

DOI: 10.4324/9781003333241-3

change our teaching or the fact that this entire experience shifted the community's culture that mattered most?

*Meet Aaron Schorn, Program Director at the Nalukai Foundation, an organization that provides leadership training to Hawai'i high school students who have an interest in technological, cultural, and social entrepreneurship. The Head of Community and Growth at Unrulr, I became acquainted with Aaron when I began using this tool for my own pedagogical documentation purposes in EDU-319, the Assessment Methods in Education course I teach at Daemen University. What I love most about Aaron is the fact that every single one of our meetings has very little to do with the tools of documentation and far more to do with the influence of documentation inside of the learning communities we create together.*

*I wasn't using Unrulr or documenting with intention on the day that Max took my breath away while story-making in our studio. I didn't understand what I was seeing, but I knew that it mattered, and I also knew that that five-year-old child had deep wisdom to share. I knew that the rest of us needed to be learning from them. I knew that we needed to listen.*

*When I began snapping photos and inviting other teachers and kids to notice what Max was doing and talk with them about it, attention turned away from me and toward Max, who was making their learning visible and teaching all of us so much. These learning moments helped us co-author something of an unexpected love story that summer: A young writer did something unexpected and wonderful—something that engaged them that we didn't understand. Their willingness to teach us, and our willingness to become students challenged our assumptions and unraveled our certainties about what writing really was and what it meant to engage and move writers well. This was when I realized that I wasn't alone in my teaching, that my students could be my mentors if I let them, and that this was how community could be built. We could build it together. What happened with Max was an accident, but it inspired a kind of intentionality that shaped our vision and the protocols I continue to rely upon in my studio and in the classrooms I teach within today.*

*And Aaron gets this.*

*"I remember when* Most Likely to Succeed, *that film about High Tech High in San Diego (Dintersmith, 2015), was released. So many people locked onto how completely*

*inconsequential the teacher seemed in those rooms," he reflected as we sank into a recent conversation about this book. "People practically fetishized the way that students moved through a class without any guidance from the teacher at all, really."*

*I remember this, too. That magic is what so many of us aim to achieve in our writing workshops and studios, and when we see that level of ownership and independence in any other context it resonates. Maybe we tend to idealize that scene because it breaks our hearts a little, too. Creating an interdependent community is tricky, and sustaining one is even harder. We marvel at it when we see it.*

*I'm a bit nostalgic about the studio that all of us created way back when Max was story-making with LEGOs. It seemed mystical, and in some ways, it might have been. Documentation helped me notice the unintentional but deeply impactful choices that all of us made during that time, though. It helped us see beneath the surface of our teaching and the relationships that were created in that space.*

*"In Hawai'i we like to talk a lot about protocols," Aaron offered, and when I revisit my documentation of that time, I see them taking shape there, even without my awareness. "You know, you enter a space and you have a protocol for entering that space. You go out on the canoe, there's a protocol for how you act. It's what we do and how we do it," Aaron said, and as someone who appreciates the power of protocols, I immediately understood him. Protocols are procedures that ensure equity. They help to establish norms. Aaron wasn't telling me anything new—I used them all of the time—but then, he shared an important "why."*

*"In the classroom, protocols are about making reflection and documentation…not… weird," he said. "Really great teachers have really great protocols, and those protocols are sacred." Right! I thought to myself, nodding vigorously. That's really what it's all about.*

*Protocols are about making documentation … not weird. You're welcome to explore some of my favorites in the appendix.*

My colleague in the room that day didn't wait for Max to produce a draft with written words in order to learn more about their story-writing prowess. Instead, she nudged me toward their table and encouraged me to pay attention to their thinking and work in process.

*"Look,"* she said. *"Listen."*

In the years that followed, I chased down protocols that made looking and listening robust and routine. They inform the way that I approach lesson studies with teachers now. Visit my digital documentation notebook to learn more and explore examples when you're ready.

Our willingness to watch and learn from Max as they made their narrative taught us so much more about them, story-making in general, and their unique writing process than merely assessing their final product could have. If you've been teaching for any length of time, I know you appreciate this, too. You've likely had similar experiences, and you may even document moments like these in some fashion. Like me, you probably value students' learning process more than the results of it. You may even speak that language often when you're reflecting on your own assessment intentions in the company of other friends in the field.

If you've picked up this particular book, I know that documentation may already be making a significant difference in the lives of the learners you serve, as it changes the way you think about teaching and, consequently, the way you teach them.

I wonder: Is it serving *you*, though?

Are you giving yourself the same permission to value the process of your own learning rather than the mere product of it? What would that look like? Why might it matter? I hope that this book equips you with processes, tools, prompts, and enough inspiration to invite documentation into your own classroom. More importantly, I hope that it invites you to make space for it in your own life—professionally and personally. Documentation is all about learning, and learning happens in so many contexts.

Here's something you might be interested to know: I nearly made the third part of this book a toolkit for coaching students to document their own learning. I decided against this in the final revisions, though. I want the whole of this book to be all about you—the teacher who is eager to fall or remain in love with their own learning, to discover how to look and listen a bit differently, to have their practices and their thinking changed, and to find themselves engaged and perhaps—rejuvenated and even restored—by this work.

I document my learning as a teacher each day. I also document it as a writer, an instructional designer, a professional learning facilitator, a parent, a wife, a friend, and a woman who has entered her third act of life. I'm in the middle of trying to figure so many things out, including learning how to live a more conscious, vibrant, and connected life. Documentation helps me understand things I wouldn't otherwise. Sometimes, in order to understand what's happening, we need to fall silent for a while. We need to look and listen, and simply capture what we see and hear—without written words. So yes, documentation has become a multimodal tool for my personal and professional learning. It's also become a tool for healing within and well beyond the spaces I teach within. Perhaps it will become a similar force in your own life.

## The Documentation Process and Why It Matters

Documentation is a process that involves making observations of learning as it happens in a single moment or over time, taking photographs, making audio or video recordings, or gathering documents and artifacts as we do so, interpreting that evidence, and then inviting others to share their perspectives about our process and the results of it before starting all over again (Making Learning Visible: Understanding, Documenting, and Supporting Individual and Group Learning, 2006). I've illustrated my own translation of this process for you in Figure 1.1 Understanding these essential elements is an important first step in becoming an effective documentarian. Consider how these steps serve as a simple illustration of what can become a far richer and more complex process if you choose.

Think about this as well: Even when your process is a simple one—perhaps you're planning to document just one bit of learning that unfolds in just one small moment—it's important to co-create that experience with those

## The Different Postures that Documentarians Assume

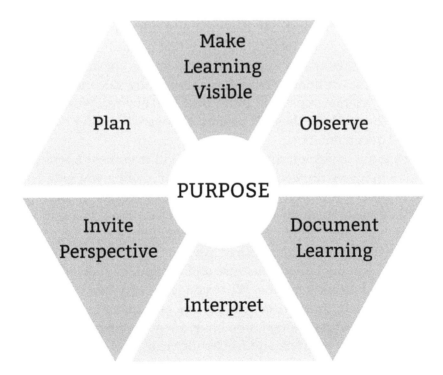

*Figure 1.1—Different Postures that Documentarians Assume*

you are learning about and from. This will ensure that those who are most impacted by the work have influence over how it's designed and that your biases are kept in better check. You'll find examples of what this might look like inside of simple and more complex processes in my digital documentation notebook.

Documentation is an assessment approach that can be used in different ways and for very different purposes. It distinguishes itself from common assessment methods that we typically encounter in schools by its potential to support more than the evaluation of learning products, though. Meaningful documentation experiences actually produce deep learning. This is about so much more than calculation, analysis, and appraisal. It's about engagement and fulfillment, and in my experience, this is something that everyone involved in the process experiences, including teachers. Documentation makes us more present practitioners. This, in itself, is a tremendous gift.

The documentation of learning reveals things that the products of it tend to obscure. It's through this process that documentarians begin to connect who they are to what they do, how they do it, and perhaps most importantly—why. Obviously, these discoveries can help us improve our learning and work, and as teachers, we are constantly reminded of our responsibilities here. I hope that you'll consider this, though: Documentation often helps us uncover surprising, simple, and even delightful solutions to problems that the field tends to complicate. When we study our learning, we teach ourselves what works, what doesn't, and why that might be happening in our specific context. This makes us better diagnosticians and interventionists. It makes us better practitioners, too. More importantly, documentation draws us into closer relationships with our students. They recognize us learning right beside them. About them. For them. These are beautiful byproducts of pedagogical documentation.

These are my hopes for you: I hope you will document learning so that you can fall in love with teaching all over again. I hope you will document learning in order to deepen your self-awareness, reclaim your confidence, and sustain your motivation for your vital work. I hope that you will find your people this way. I hope you will create and hold spaces for one another where curiosity, vibrancy, and delight persist. You will have to commit to noticing what you might not otherwise and recognizing how significant the seemingly insignificant might be. What you learn may often encourage and even enchant you. If I'm being honest, documentation has left me bewildered and even frustrated just as often, though. It often heightens our experiences, intensifying the way we think and feel about them, too.

When we document in the company of others, we widen the lens through which we observe any environment and the people and objects within it.

My daughter Laura taught me this when we were on a family vacation to Washington, D.C. and Philadelphia in 2008. My husband, a huge history buff, was in his element wandering slowly through each museum and lingering over every display. By the third day of this, our girl was growing restless and so, I handed her my camera.

"You get to take all of the photos for our scrapbook today," I told her. "Try to notice what matters and what we might miss if you weren't paying good attention for all of us."

By day's end, my memory card was overflowing with images I wouldn't have thought to collect: Shadowy streets and cobblestone corners, brownstones lined with tidy window boxes, vertical gardens, and a collection of clouds. It struck me—how Laura saw these cities, what she chose to remember of them, and especially, how those photos defined those places and that time for me.

The act of focusing our attention, making keen observations, and gathering evidence and artifacts engages us in the moment. It also deepens our appreciation of what is happening and, more importantly, what it might mean. When we share our documentation with others, we add texture to their interpretation of similar events or, perhaps, an entirely new take on a shared experience. So yes, documentation is a process, and as Aaron suggests, it's also a culture.

*Angelique Thompson, co-author of* The Gift of Playful Learning: A Guide for Educators *(Shell Education, 2023) and an Early Years Reading Coach in the Toronto District School Board, remembers the moment when she was confident that documentation had begun shaping the culture of the classrooms she served in.*

*"I'd created these conditions in the environment where kids would do something and then call me over. 'Okay, now take my picture,' they would say. 'I did this, and I really want you to take my picture. Will you take it? Now?'"*

*Their eagerness to document their learning was evidence of Angelique's growth as a documentarian. It was clear that some very essential habits and ways of thinking had taken root. I'm reminded of Aaron Schorn's litmus, mentioned earlier in this chapter: Documentation wasn't weird, and that's because Angelique created reliable protocols and consistent conditions that built and sustained good habits. As she reflected on the data gathered, an important tension began to build from this beginning.*

*"I began to look at all of these pictures the kids asked me to take, and wonder:* Okay, what's this even all about?" *Angelique said. "Did the images simply represent the products of learning, or did they truly serve as stories that made the process of that learning visible?"*

*Defining documentation as a story positions Angelique differently inside of the work now. "I always ask myself, 'Why are you capturing this? What's the purpose? What are you offering with this? What's the story behind this offering?' It's not necessarily what you capture, right? It's the story that matters."*

*As a storymaker, Angelique takes care to slow the moments down even as they are unfolding. This helps her notice when characters, settings, and scenes shift. She tries to capture the best of each before the next one unfolds. Rather than simply snapping images of learning products, she's better able to document the whole of the process when she frames it as a narrative and aims to gather enough evidence to fill an entire coherent storyboard. Try this perhaps, and see if Angelique's approach works for you.*

Documentation also humanizes us by sharpening our perception, enabling us to better understand, respect, and ultimately, nurture, those we seek to serve. This is work that civilizes us. It can clarify problems and help us define solutions, to be sure, and that's important. But documentation can make us a more empathetic and even affectionate people. It can heal us and even repair relationships if we're open to that. That's something that we don't talk about enough.

Teaching is fraught with tension. Each day presents us with countless dilemmas inside of systems that tend to compartmentalize knowledge and the people who possess it. As the development of the sciences has become increasingly disciplinary, so too has our thinking, our learning, and the conclusions that we draw about both. Fear has flatlined us, and our rapid and constant access to information has overloaded our brains. It's no wonder that we've come to rely upon quantitative data so much. Points, percentages, and letter grades are seemingly sturdy and sensible things, and when we thread them into theories, they help us feel like we understand incredibly complex people and phenomena that can never be quantified. Understanding demands far more from us than the simple disaggregation of surface data might reveal. Each discipline, like the humans who engage with it, invites and inspires emotion as much as it does rationality. Each invites divergence and imagination as much as it calls participants to converge and draw conclusions. Each has its own aesthetic, regardless of how comforting we find its austerity, and as Lella Gandini, Lynne Hill, Louise Cadwell, and Charles

Schwall, the authors of *In the Spirit of the Studio: Learning from the "Atelier" of Reggio Emilia* (2015), remind us, when we separate these parts of any discipline from the whole, we do more than merely diminish it—we transform it into something it is not. When we reduce human beings to subjects who behave well inside of spreadsheets, we transform learning and learners into what they are not as well (p. 18).

## The Affordances of Multimodal Memory Keeping

When I revisit the photographs, recordings, and artifacts I kept from those years that Max spent making and writing with us, I still find myself uncovering details that I hadn't noticed before, especially when I remix my pictures and recordings and bump them up against artifacts from my most recent learning experiences. Situating an image of their work taken over a decade ago beside the notes I made about another learner made while I was teaching just last week surfaces new and interesting questions about the influence of materials on the shape of his writing ideas back then and the students I'm serving now. Pictures reveal much that written words cannot, and when I listen to the audio I captured during a conversation with Max about their process, I hear something in their voice and word choice that images and print failed to render quite as well. There is certainty in their tone that was missing when they first began writing with us. There is confidence that wasn't there before. And when I place these data beside the work that eventually emerged from his process, my understanding of its quality and how Max achieved it feels far more substantial, somehow.

While many data-minded educators struggle to value the expressive potential of multimodal assessment, those of us who are committed to documentation understand the critical role that it plays in creating and sustaining our individual and shared identities. While so many assessment efforts strive to simplify problems and produce rapid and tidy conclusions, documentation challenges us to make the experience of understanding learning far more complex as it provides us the tools to remember, revisit, and rethink it. Too many treat multimodal expression as superfluous rather than essential, but if we agree that the whole of any learning story cannot be reduced to a percentage or a number, we could also agree that each mode of expression affords learners something that the others may not, and that if we're to truly understand ourselves and one another, we need to consider as much of the whole of those stories as possible. Moments are fleeting, but documentation helps us curate them well, or at the very least, better. Numbers, percentages—quantitative data of all kinds—would have us believe that learning is a predictable, rational animal. It's quite a bit messier than that, though. Learning can be rational, even as it is emotional. It's the stuff of fact and fiction, reality and imagination, ugliness and beauty. It's as pedantic as it is artistic, as aesthetic as it is often dull, and even, at times, unappealing. When we fail to document as much of the whole of this as we possibly can, we fail to retell the whole of the story, and then the conclusions and themes that surface from the experience are not merely incomplete—they're dishonest.

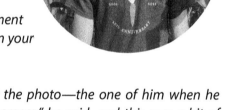

*When I spoke with sixteen-year-old homeschooled student Silence Karl about his affinity for documentation, he told me about a photo he recently saw of himself. "My mom's feeling a bit nostalgic about me growing up lately, and so we've been digging through old photo albums," he admits quietly, and I smile.*

*"My daughter is moving into her first apartment at the end of the month," I tell him. "Go easy on your mom."*

*And he laughs before telling me more about the photo—the one of him when he wasn't even five years old. "I was holding a camera," he said, and this was a bit of foreshadowing. "That's always been my favorite way to tell stories."*

*Silence knows how to write—really well. He enjoys it, too. "But I go out into the world looking for a scene," he says. When I ask him how he knows he's found a good one, he offers a one-word response. "Emotion," he offers with certainty. "Wherever there's emotion, there's something to capture there."*

*This is a theme that resonates through my conversations with Angelique and Aaron as well, and it leaves me wondering this: What if documentation were a culture, and what if doing it wasn't weird, and what if the way we went about it was much like story-making? What if we went searching for scenes worth capturing by becoming increasingly sensitive to emotion? What if that shifts in mood were an indicator of learning processes unfolding? How might this further humanize the entire experience?*

All of this said, I know from experience how impossible it is to document every experience, or even a handful of them, some days. When I was in the classroom, I had upward of 120 students each year, and class periods were as short as 27 and no more than 43 minutes long each day. While I was fortunate to work with a co-teacher and we were inclined to document our learning despite the fact that we were not well aware of the practice I plan to share in this book, our effort was hardly consistent or sophisticated. We relied on grades, and our content was the sun that our students orbited around. If this is your dynamic, I hope this book shifts something for you. When learning is centered, documentation becomes a necessary part of it, and the classroom becomes less of a solar system and instead, something that looks more like an interdependent network. Each learner becomes a node within it. Information is carried back and forth across this system, evolving as it moves and powers the network. In an age when information is abundant and immediately accessible, what's known about any one thing is constantly shape-shifting. Teachers who understand this know that sustaining that energy and strengthening the connection between the nodes in any learning system is critical to learning.

Documentation saves us from the simple stories we tell ourselves about our efforts to make that happen. It challenges us to look beyond the superficial, and it reminds us, especially when we've shifted into auto drive, that what's happening in our classrooms is rich and textured and complicated, even when it doesn't appear this way on the surface. Documentation also reminds us that often, our dissatisfaction with our work and relationships is a defense mechanism. We disconnect because we're overwhelmed. We automate decisions, practices, and behaviors in order to better manage each moment. Documentation invites us to notice and wonder again. It invites us to pay attention and then look a bit closer and differently, too. It allows us to use just-the-right tools at just-the-right times, in order to capture and remember just-the-right moments that remind us of the full catastrophe—the moments that make us and the learners we serve whole.

## It's the Mixture of Modes That Matters

It was the pedagogistas in Reggio Emilia, Italy, who taught me about the language of paper. "It's different from clay," one of them explained, smiling as she gestured toward a towering documentation panel that featured the work of young writers beside their reflections on that work (Mori, 2019). When we speak about multimodality, we refer to visual, aural, gestural, spatial, alphabetic, and haptic expressions. These are the modes through which human beings communicate, and each possesses affordances that the others do not. Written words reveal something that sound cannot. Gesture reveals what vibration is unable to, and images allow us to see what cannot be expressed in other ways. All expression is multimodal in nature. It's always been this way, and yet, when individualists created schools where other individualists could be successful, they privileged the written word in ways that maintain its—and their—power (Hammond, 2015). This has done immeasurable and in many ways irreparable harm, and we need to look no further than the ways in which we tend to define and measure learning to prove this theory.

Numbers, letters, and percentages shore up a great deal of false confidence around theories that emerge from shallow stories. Certainty matters to be sure, but whenever I'm beginning to feel as if I can no longer be humbled, I try to recognize that shift for what it is: A red flag. A warning. A reminder to recognize and honor the conclusions that I or others have drawn but also an invitation to document the learning that's still happening even as conclusions are being drawn. Learning stories cannot be reduced to what we've merely seen or heard in any single or handful of contexts. Gesture reveals what paper cannot. Images speak a thousand words. Listening teaches us what our eyes cannot see. Each mode of expression has a language of its own, and when we connect them, we deepen our understanding of learners and learning. When we connect one mode of expression to another inside of a documentation experience, each is elevated. As Jody Shipka, the author of *Toward a Composition Made Whole* (2011) suggests, multimodality makes stories and the humans we build stories around a bit more complete. This is what makes documentation beautiful, and it's this beauty that saves us all from the superficial stories that diminish our theories about learners and learning.

If you're reading this book, then you are likely an educator who likely appreciates expressive languages, or at the very least, has some awareness of what they are. You appreciate how multimodality makes learning and teaching far more textured and whole. You recognize its potential to make content more accessible and communication far more creative and even culturally considerate. You might also recognize how multimodal documentation can make assessment more efficient and how it can save us abundant time. This is possible when we aren't constantly bringing learning to a halt in order to test the mastery of its discrete elements.

## Preparing to Document by Examining Your Convictions

Before I could ever reap the rewards of pedagogical documentation, I had to get clear about the convictions I carried around about teaching and learning. I had to begin thinking differently about the environment I created and even protected in my classroom, too. I had to let go of a few assumptions that weren't serving anyone very well. To be honest, I still find them at work under the surface of nearly every less-than-satisfying experience that plagues me, regardless of the role that I might be playing at the time. For instance, it's easy to assume that our assessments are reliable and valid—especially the ones we've been careful to design ourselves. We might believe that all good teachers are experts, infallible, or beyond reproach. When learners struggle, we might feel especially responsible for this. We might even take pity on them or approach them as flawed people in need of repair. We might treat learning as something that can be quantified. We might pay far more attention to deficits rather than strengths—in any or even most contexts.

It's important for you to know that I'm hardly impervious to the pull of these misperceptions. I just recognize them for what they are, now: Red flags that indicate that my energy or skills might be lacking. When I find myself thinking this way with increased regularity, I know that it's time to rest, reset, and enlist some helpers. It was my most humbling experience that helped me develop that important bit of self-awareness.

### TLDR (Too Long Didn't Read)

As I mentioned in the introduction, you'll find a section just like this one at the end of each chapter. My intention is to give you a bite-sized summary of what you might eventually go back and linger over in the future, or perhaps serve as a reminder of something you read closely in the past but have since forgotten. I hope this helps you traverse this text with purpose and ease. Remember, it's not necessary to read it cover-to-cover. Treat it like a toolkit. Pull what you need when you need it. Use each TLDR section to reorient yourself as needed, skim, and choose what you'll explore or try. I want to give a shout out to Emily and Amelia Nagoski here, too. They're the authors of *Burnout: The Secret to Unlocking the Stress Cycle* (2019) and the first to introduce me to an end-of-chapter TLDR section. I loved it as a reader, and they've inspired my writing now, too.

1. Documentation involves making a plan, making learning visible, observing, taking photos, capturing audio and video recordings, or gathering artifacts of learning, and interpreting the evidence gathered.
2. Documentation helps us understand those we hope to serve better. It helps us understand ourselves better, too.
3. Documentation is a multimodal experience, and multimedia tools help us capture what written words and numbers alone cannot. This makes the stories we tell about learners and learning more complete.

4.  Documentation is often more rewarding when we're sensitive to the ways in which it shifts our perspectives about learning and assessment. Deepening our awareness of these beliefs and remaining open to changing them is an important part of becoming a documentarian.
5.  Documentation heightens experiences, and it also tends to deepen our enthusiasm and passion for learning. These are wonderful side-effects that can also contribute to bias. We must be intentional about engaging the people we aim to understand through documentation as co-designers of our processes. We should also take care to seek diverse perspectives throughout the work—especially from those whose identities are different from our own.
6.  Documentation is a process that changes the cultures it is conducted within.

## Let's Reflect

Before you begin planning in earnest, sit with these questions for a while:

Where are you noticing incomplete stories in your own life or in the learning and work that you do beside your students?

How might documentation help you better understand yourself or others?

How might you plan to mitigate bias in your own documentation work?

## Try This: Just Right Tools and Invitations

### Document and Interpret a Moment

Use the process illustrated in Figure 1.1 to plan a micro-project. Document a single moment of joy, surprise, discovery, relief, satisfaction, connection, course, or release in your personal or professional experience. Then, make a simple interpretation: What happened in that moment, and how did it change your feelings or perspective?

### Document and Interpret a Journey

If you'd like a greater challenge, document and interpret three distinct personal or professional moments when you recognize a shift in your own mood. Then, make a deeper interpretation: What happened within each moment, and how did each event shift your thoughts or feelings? When you look across these moments, what patterns or juxtapositions do you notice?

**Document and Interpret an Expedition**

Dive into any of the digital or physical photo albums you've maintained for some time—months or perhaps even years. Try to identify what you were noticing in single moments and images. Then, study a bunch of them at once. What is this revealing to you about your own interests, affinities, or passions? What patterns are you noticing in your work over time? What stories are missing? Whose?

# References

Dintersmith, T. (2015). *Most Likely to Succeed*. EDU21C Foundation. Retrieved June 28, 2023, from https://www.amazon.com/Most-Likely-Succeed-Brian-Cesson/dp/B07F7ZQRQQ#:~:text=Most%20Likely%20to%20Succeed%20examines,teachers%20are%20capable%20of%20doing

Gandini, L., Hill, L., Boyd Cadwell, L., & Schwall, C. S. (2015). *In the spirit of the studio: Learning from the "atelier" of Reggio Emilia*. Teachers College Press.

Hammond, Z. (2015). *Culturally responsive teaching and the brain: Promoting authentic engagement and rigor among culturally and linguistically diverse students*. Corwin.

Nagoski, E., & Nagoski, A. (2020). *Burnout: The secret to unlocking the stress cycle*. Ballantine Books.

Shipka, J. (2011). *Toward a composition made whole* (Ser. Pittsburgh series in composition, literacy, and culture). University of Pittsburgh Press.

Stockman, A. M. (2019, February 18). *Conversation with Marina Mori. personal*.

Thompson, A., & Bynoe, N. K. (2023). *The gift of playful learning: A guide for educators*. Shell Education Publishing.

# 2

# What Brings You Here?

Max wasn't the first young writer who inspired me to document my learning. There were dozens of writers who'd come before them who compelled me. For instance, long before there was Max, there was that student in my eighth-grade class who wasn't producing any writing for me but whose mother met me after class one afternoon with stacks of her notebooks in hand. Her daughter was a prolific writer outside of school, she told me. She loved Stephanie Meyers's *Twilight* (2005), and it inspired volumes of fan fiction. I'm remembering the "keepers" file I kept in my desk drawer when I was teaching seniors, too. Inside were notes I gathered during writing conferences that spring. We were writing iSearch papers (Macrorie, 1988), and their struggles were as interesting to me as the successes they were finding. I kept copies of their process work beside final drafts and 35 mm photographs that remind me of this time.

When I founded my writing studio in 2008, I began taking photos more consistently. There are dozens of digital albums in my Google Drive now, filled to the brim with evidence of our collective learning, the evolution of different spaces that we made our own over the years, and the contributions that other teachers and authors made to our learning. As I revisit these images, recordings, and artifacts, I have an even greater appreciation for what I was doing: I was documenting to remember. And because I made that commitment way back then, I'm continuing to learn new things from documentation even now, nearly twenty years later.

We document what is meaningful, authentic, and compelling within a specific context—minutes or hours, days or weeks, months, or even years.

DOI: 10.4324/9781003333241-4

Our purposes for documenting learning are varied, and it's not uncommon to feel pulled in different directions as we begin and then become more practiced in this work.

As a young teacher, I documented to remember the moments that moved me and the ones that moved my students, too. I documented our joy, our successes, and, most of all, our affection for one another. I wanted to remember these moments. Maybe you do, too. Do that. It matters. And you should also know this: Documenting to remember joy in one moment prepares you to document for other terrifically cerebral purposes later on. Those images and recordings and artifacts you collect in order to remember one small and moving moment might eventually live beside others that are gathered later on in your career for very different reasons. When you revisit them in that context, they will help you discover things you may not have otherwise. You might uncover new possibilities this way. Better solutions. Promising practices.

## Moments, Journeys, and Expeditions

I've documented peeks into a writer's process by taking photos as she created just the very beginning of an argument. I've audio-recorded feedback offered to a storymaker as I walked the room during independent writing time, and I've captured video recordings of mini-lessons. Reflecting on these moments deepened my learning, for sure. Sometimes, I document moments in order to simply remember them, though—like that moment during last week's Assessment Methods class when I scrambled to capture the playful banter that erupted when my students were creating learning walls, inspired by Jessica Vance, teacher, coach, and author of *Leading with a Lens of Inquiry: Cultivating Conditions for Curiosity and Empowering Agency* (2022). I never want to forget that moment. You can read more about this in my digital documentation notebook, referenced in the third part of this book.

I've also documented different series of moments that felt a bit more like a journey. I'm reminded of when my students began experimenting with sticky notes in my writing studio long before anyone was blogging or reeling about them on Instagram. It started slowly when one of them asked if she could use our massive whiteboard to plot her novel. As others looked on, they became intrigued by her approach and began to riff off of it. Soon, sticky notes were an essential resource, and not because they were fun to work with, but because they were helping writers do their work more creatively and efficiently. It was young writers who taught me how sticky notes simultaneously ease the process while elevating the quality of our ideas and the words we eventually produce. I spent several months capturing the many varied ways they were using them in an effort to understand their utility for different kinds of writers and, more importantly, the potential they held for all of us. You can read that learning story in my digital documentation notebook too, if you'd like.

More than this, I've studied how varied journeys have contributed to entire expeditions that continue to unfold over the course of months or even years. My early documentation efforts weren't nearly as intentional as those I make today, and I love thinking about how completely organic they were. I took those photos and captured those videos and kept those artifacts because they represented simple but poignant experiences. Once I became far more purposeful about documenting learning, I thought I was merely assessing progress toward learning goals, chasing problems to solve, or gathering evidence that could help me improve my practice. These are worthy purposes, to be sure, but as I return to those images, recordings, and artifacts now, I realize that the entire practice of documentation was so much messier and far more complicated than this.

*Aaron reminds me that when we shift from documenting moments to documenting journeys, we become far more metacognitive in our work. Perhaps this is why the work starts to feel quite a bit less efficient the deeper we move into it. When we make this thinking visible to students, this changes our relationship with them, too. Teachers are not perceived to be all-knowing experts in communities that nurture pedagogical documentation.*

*"The teacher is part of the collective here," he tells me. "Students are teaching other students, and they're teaching the teacher, too."*

*This changes the classic distribution of power that we tend to find in schools, disrupting what Paolo Freire likened to a banking model of education where teachers were treated as wealthy donors who deposited knowledge into the minds of students who were likened to empty vessels (Freire, 1972). In interdependent communities where teachers and students alike position themselves as learners and thinking is made visible, documented, and analyzed, it's far more common to recognize the different funds of knowledge that individuals bring to the collective. No one is an empty vessel, wealthy donors are less necessary, and power is better distributed.*

# The Documentation Kaleidoscope

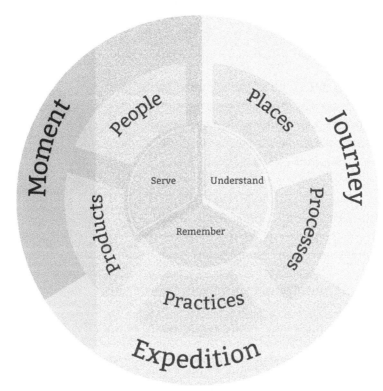

*Figure 2.1—The Documentation Kaleidoscope*

The camera may position us for straight-on seeing, but each image is much like a single tile inside a multi-textured, tumbling kaleidoscope that mesmerizes but can also confound us. I've tried to illustrate this in Figure 2.1. Take a moment to steady this contraption before you begin tilting it toward your unique learning landscaping and twisting the tube for effect. Know that each time you return to this book, you'll choose to document a moment, a journey, or an entire expedition yourself. You'll do so to remember what happened, to better understand someone or something, or to serve yourself or others well. You'll capture what you notice about people, places, processes, practices, and the products of learning along the way.

If you've been documenting learning for any length of time, then you know how fleeting any instance worth capturing can be. Perhaps this is why I'm so drawn to this discipline, and maybe it's the reason why you might be, too. Documentation is playful. It feels much like a scavenger hunt, and when I'm in documentation mode, I can feel my senses awaken. Documentation requires a willingness to be surprised by what I might discover, ever-attentive, and quick on the draw. While this can feel uncomfortable from time to time, I know that it's this heightened sense of anticipation and possibility that keeps me curious and hungry to learn more. Documentation preserves my young-teacher energy. It keeps my heart and my mind engaged in my work, especially when the circumstances are less than ideal.

*"As new documentarians, it's not uncommon for us to snap! Snap! Snap! our way through a learning moment by capturing products of learning," Kenisha Bynoe recently reflected, as I spoke with her while drafting this book. Co-author of* The Gift of Playful Learning *(2023), a French Immersion Educator, and an Early Reading Coach for the Toronto District School Board, Kenisha shares the wisdom of experience. As beginners, we're not quite sure how to document learning as it unfolds.*

*"Sometimes, I took a lot of pictures of the very same thing, only from slightly different angles, and when I went back to reflect, I couldn't really remember why I took a certain photo or what it was about."*

*It was a mentor who helped shift her practice in deeply satisfying ways.*

*"I took Additional Qualification courses with Darlene Avis-Pottinger who is now a Toronto District School Board Principal. She taught us what learning stories were and how we could slow the process of capturing thinking down by paying close attention and observing what children said, what they did, and what they were representing." Darlene coached Kenisha to remain present in each moment and to strive to be in tune with the children she was learning from so that she could find the thread of the narrative that was unfolding in front of her. "Whatever we collected would need to tell a story about how the learning happened over time," she said. "So, I started capturing what learners said, what they did, and what they created in order to represent their ideas."*

*Eventually, these images, recordings, and annotations could be hung together, much like a storyboard, so that those who weren't in the room like family members could better understand learners by revisiting their processes.*

*Kenisha's story should inspire those of you who already distinguish the documentation of a moment from a journey or an expedition. How might you slow the moments down, notice what learners say, do, and create, and use various documentation postures and tools to capture the whole of that story, whether it unfolds in a single moment or over time?*

## What's Motivating You?

Perhaps you've come to this text with a clear purpose. You might have a problem in hand—one you'd like to solve. Or maybe you're interested in a far more deductive process that will help you uncover new possibilities. You can certainly approach your learning and work this way.

You may be a beginner who is just becoming attuned to your own purposes and practices, and that's okay. We all start small, and as we come to know our subjects, tools, materials, and the landscape that we're working within, documentation will become more than a habit we've developed a discipline around. For many of you, documentation may become a deep, personal need that you must fulfill. If you're a seasoned documentarian, then you might agree that, despite your experience, the work remains messy and uncertain. I still feel confused and even frustrated after many days. Documentation is hard and humbling. It's made me comfortable with discomfort, though. It's also tiring, but as someone who is relatively acclimatized to this way of being now, it feels a bit more synchronized. It's easier to enter a state of flow, and when the intensity of any documentation effort is over, the rewards are always worth that effort.

Are you a beginner? Then you may want to start by documenting single moments: Learning that happens in one place at one time. Those small experiences may inspire a greater journey: A series of single moments that unfold over days or weeks. Journeys may help you discover the unexpected or better understand the phenomena you notice within a single moment. If, like me, you're an experienced documentarian and you're seeking fresh perspective and new motivations for your work, you might relate to my earlier reflection and use this book to pursue a similar purpose: Reflect on your documentation to uncover the essential questions, conundrums, and curiosities that have been a sustaining force inside your work over months, years, or even decades. Continue to document for that greater purpose, even as you capture and then reflect on the smaller moments and journeys that help you understand and serve yourself and others well in very specific contexts.

Whenever I'm feeling overwhelmed, documenting simple moments centers me. I'm currently reading Cyndie Spiegel's Microjoys: *Finding Hope (Especially) When Life is Not Okay* (2023). Here, she shares her experiences with profound and unrelenting trauma, and the healing influence of simply noticing and naming ordinary, daily delights. I find that routine matters very much, too. Documentation brings the best of these practices together in a way that can sustain us. Sometimes, documentation isn't about imagining what can be. Sometimes, it's about acknowledging what is. Holding it closer. Recommitting instead of letting go.

*My friend Lisa Green has taught me much about how our purposes for documentation shift as we grow into the work. A second-grade teacher from West Valley Central School District in western New York State, I've had the privilege of learning beside Lisa for several years now. She began documenting her learning a few years ago when her school district adopted a new curriculum that did not include any on-demand tasks that generated grades.*

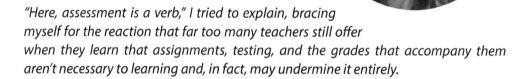

*"Here, assessment is a verb," I tried to explain, bracing myself for the reaction that far too many teachers still offer when they learn that assignments, testing, and the grades that accompany them aren't necessary to learning and, in fact, may undermine it entirely.*

*But I'd underestimated Lisa and all of her colleagues, too. This was refreshing news, and they were excited by the potential it might have to improve classroom and even school culture. When I showed Lisa my documentation notebook that same day, she dove headlong into her learning about pedagogical documentation and began capturing moments and then soon enough entire learning journeys. I can say with confidence now that Lisa is on a sustained learning expedition.*

*"I really began documenting my learning because our new curriculum didn't include assignments or quizzes or tests," she remembers. "I needed a way to assess without those things, and you showed me how you document what you learn from making assessments of children in your notebook. I remember I was just intrigued."*

*And so, she tried.*

*Lisa began documenting her students' progress toward learning goals in single moments at first. "And this really made me evaluate what I was doing as a teacher. When you document, you are constantly wondering, 'What's my purpose here? What am I really focusing on in my lesson? What am I hoping they will learn or be able to do?'"*

*Lisa explains that early on, pedagogical documentation made her a far more reflective teacher and someone who really began to understand her state learning standards better. "I realized that we all interpret them a bit differently too," she said. "Documentation showed me what I value when it comes to those standards, how I interpret them, and what's most important about them."*

*I explain that I'm one who has invited groups of teachers to document the way they teach and assess standards-based learning targets in the past, and when we put these artifacts—these data—next to one another, so much is revealed about the existence of alignment, teachers' diverse perspectives about practice, where those differences serve learners, and where confusions or even flaws exist. Documentation helps us design better curriculum and assessments. It helps us make far better instructional decisions, too. In my experience, I tell Lisa, performance doesn't improve unless we're documenting and reflecting on what we learn from students in process. Tests, quizzes, worksheets, and other products of learning aren't as helpful. We typically have plenty of that kind of data anyway. We need to better understand how learners are thinking and how what we're doing is serving or convoluting that.*

*"Right," Lisa nods on her side of the screen. "And because I became so much more conscious of my purposes early on, documentation raised all of these questions for me." It made Lisa more inquisitive. It wasn't long before she grew beyond documenting moments deductively to documenting a journey in a far more inductive way. Lisa will tell this story later on in this book, but I wanted to introduce her here because she's a very bright light in my documentation world, and this has everything to do with how generous she is about sharing her growth as a documentarian. She's a perfect example of someone who consistently recommits to her learning and her work instead of letting go entirely.*

*This trait was put to the test this year, too. Lisa became a documentarian as a kindergarten teacher with a small group of students. Her potential to document well shifted dramatically as she became a second-grade teacher to a much bigger class. She wasn't able to document as often or as extensively over the last year. And while she assured me that she isn't quitting, she was realistic about what's possible in this context, what isn't, and what could change. Perhaps Lisa is not going to be able to document progress toward every learning target or standard in nearly every subject area she teaches now. Perhaps she'll return to documenting moments for very specific purposes instead. Maybe this will help her get her legs beneath her again and then gain a different kind of traction and find a different rhythm, she tells me. And I have no doubt that it will. Lisa realizes that documentation is a way of being now. It's an expedition that will continue to unfold over the course of her career. There will be turbulence, pauses, and unexpected detours along the way. She seems to understand this and is not only comfortable with that reality but also excited about what it will teach her.*

## Inviting Company, Finding Critical Friends, and Considering Positionality

I've learned much about the concept of positionality from the generous work of the Indigenous Initiatives at the Center for Teaching, Learning, and Technology at the University of British Columbia (n.d.). It's a term that acknowledges the way in which social positions and power differentials shape our identities and societal access. Misawa (2010, p. 26) speaks to the evolving and relational aspects of social identity formation, reminding us that our identities are molded by our socially defined positions and affiliations, which are deeply ingrained in our societal system.

In a more methodological approach, Duarte (2017, p. 135), a Pascua Yaqui/Chicana scholar, explains positionality as an approach requiring researchers to recognize their own privilege levels in terms of race, class, education level, income, ability, gender, and citizenship among others. This process helps them examine and act from their social position in a world laden with injustice.

When we recognize our positionality, we simultaneously notice the interplay of various social identities and intricate power dynamics, and we ground our teaching and learning in an understanding of intersectionality. This concept, rooted in Black feminist legal studies and critical race theories, deals with the ways in which various forms of oppression, such as race and gender or sexuality and nation, intersect. As Hill Collins (2001) and Kimberlé W. Crenshaw (2017) point out, intersectionality reminds us that oppression cannot be narrowed down to a single type and that different forms of oppression collaborate in creating injustice.

Many of us document in order to connect with others, engage in collaborative meaning-making, and share our learning and the products of it with a far wider community. When we invite others into our process, we build collective energy and wisdom. More importantly, inviting diverse perspectives also helps us notice our positionality and check our biases, too. As you consider your own purposes for documentation, think about the colleagues within and well beyond your immediate world who might bring different and powerful lenses to your work. Determine who your critical friends might be as well.

Critical friends are supporters who champion our learning by offering feedback that helps us grow. They speak openly, candidly, and constructively about the flaws in our design, processes, and the conclusions we're drawing. They challenge us to approach problems directly and lean into emotionally charged issues in an informed, honest, and empathetic way. Critical friends help us consider the unintended consequences of the choices we might make as documentarians. It was a critical friend who inspired me to think differently and perhaps better about the potentially harmful consequences of making our documentation efforts and work shareable.

My first experiences with documentation found me eagerly capturing images, recordings, and artifacts and then displaying them in ways that drew a crowd. I wanted them to help me interpret them. Whether I was creating documentation panels inside of my writing studio or the classrooms I was working in or building digital albums that my wider learning network could access, I learned from experience that the rewards of inviting company into my process were immeasurable. I noticed things I would not have otherwise, deepened collegial connections, and began decentering myself more and more often within my work. Whenever I invited others to document, reflect, and make meaning beside me I became far more conscious of my positionality within the work. I noticed how my social orientation within the group and the power I maintained influenced the shape of the project, the choices I made within it, and the conclusions that I was reaching. I also began to realize, with help from my own critical friends, that it wasn't my place to share images, recordings, or artifacts that the subjects of my study produced, even if their stories were contributing to my own learning. I needed permission, and even with it, I needed to remember that permission given in one moment might be something that a learner wishes they could rescind in another. Context matters, and when it comes to sharing our documentation and the learning stories that emerge from it, our comfort level shifts dramatically as time passes and audiences, settings, and climate change. It's for this reason that I am discriminating about what I choose to share online, whom I invite into spaces where deep documentation work is happening, and which stories I include in any of my publications. You will want to be intentional here as well. If you're uncertain how to find and engage critical friends, Chapter 8 may be of particular interest to you.

I wonder: How will you position yourself within your next documentation project? Can you appreciate the importance of protecting students' privacy and their rights to choose what will be shared about them? Can you appreciate how, even when permission is given at one moment in time, learners' feelings may shift as the context in which their stories are shared changes? How will this influence the choices you make right now as you contemplate your next documentation project?

As I wrestled with all of these tensions myself, my friend Dr. Ann Marie Luce introduced me to the Photovoice method. It may be one that you wish to consider as you begin to define the best approaches for your work. Shaped by Pablo Freire's theory of critical consciousness (1974), the spirit of participatory documentary photography, and feminist perspectives, Photovoice distinguishes itself from other documentation efforts in a few significant ways. First, this method raises the critical consciousness of all participants and those who are informed by their findings by positioning the subjects as the documentarians and storytellers. This invites the creation of what Amanda O. Latz refers to as counterstories, or stories that tend to diverge from common or popular narratives. Photovoice strives to center the subjects who are being documented by honoring and elevating their expertise. Often, these are adults and children who live and learn on the margins. Historically, their stories are often documented and shared by privileged researchers who do not share their experiences, possess their insights, or own their expertise. Photovoice positions such researchers as potential allies and advocates within the learning community instead, challenging them to leverage their positionality and power in service to those documentarians whose stories need to reach the policymakers and leaders who have the power to influence change (Latz, 2017).

While I am no expert in Photovoice methodology, elements of this practice have inspired my own documentation work over the years, and in the summer of 2022, I began my first Photovoice project with the young writers in my studio and several students in my Assessment Methods course at Daemen University. This was experimental and imperfect work. Still, I learned a great deal that was not at all expected, much of it relating to how I invite learners to communicate their learning stories, where I am still struggling to get this right, and how we determine who would benefit most from hearing those stories once they're ready to be shared. If you're interested in taking a quick detour, those reflections might be worth exploring. You'll find them in my digital documentation notebook, beside the stories shared by my teacher friends and documentarians Dr. Julie Johnson, Mandy Robek, and Danielle Hardt. These women worked beside me through this process, documenting our journey, and helping me notice much that I wouldn't otherwise, along the way.

*"So much of who we are shows up in our pedagogical documentation approach,"* Angelique reflected *when we had the opportunity to catch up on Zoom as I was drafting this book. "I grew up with siblings who learned in very different ways, and so I've always known that it was my job to offer learning opportunities that would actually tap into difference."*

*Multimodal expression matters here. Communication is not limited to the production or consumption of written or even spoken words. Children build, draw, and gesture. The smallest body movements reveal shifts in their thinking and their emotions. When we allow a full range of expression, we're better able to make informed assessments that are far more strengths based.*

*"There are so many ways for children to show their thinking," Angelique agrees. "Pedagogical documentation helps me tap into their brilliance."*

*Think about this as you experiment with the Documentation Kaleidoscope. Consider your purposes for documentation as well as what or who you intend to capture. Then, try to choose dynamic tools that will allow you to document shifts in expressive mode. For instance, photographs help us capture visual and spatial products of learning well, while video and audio capture oral and gestural expressions best. I often find myself relying on both in a single moment of documentation, and that's why my cell phone is one of my favorite documentation tools. We'll explore tools and their potential more in Chapter 6.*

## Finding Your Footing

I know that each time you dip into this text, your needs and interests may be different. You will be different, too. My own commitment to documentation has helped me notice how I've grown and changed over time. For instance, as I was preparing to write this book, I spent a lot of time digging through photos and artifacts of learning captured many years ago. I'm interpreting these data differently now, and this is because I've changed. My vision is not only sharper, but I'm noticing new shapes and colors each time I peer into my kaleidoscope. I'm tracing interesting patterns and discovering uncommon connections, too.

Do you notice the same as an experienced documentarian, or are these new and intriguing possibilities for you? I wonder: How might you use this book to deepen your relationship with documentation, regardless of your history with it? I never imagined, when I first began documenting my learning, how my relationship with it would change so dramatically over time. It means something different and so much more to me now, as I look back over an incredibly rewarding career that also presented me with countless frustrations, disappointments, and dead-ends. Much has been uncertain and even unfair. I rarely made the difference I truly wanted to make for any student or teacher, if I'm being honest. And I know that I'm not alone with these feelings, either. Yet, when I sift through these prized photographs and run my eyes over the annotations I furiously scribbled across a notebook page, I'm reminded of how much this learning has always mattered to me. When I listen to my conferences with countless young writers, I hear how wholehearted our exchanges are. I remember them. I remember us. Looking back at it all, I notice the gifts tucked into each experience—the rewards that often went unrecognized as I was wrestling with the tensions of the day-to-day. I want all of this for you, too. Perhaps more than anything else.

Visit the appendix to complete a self-assessment that can help you establish a vision for your learning and work as a documentarian. You'll determine whether you will document in order to remember, understand, or better serve people, places, practices, processes, or products of learning. Then, you'll consider whether your initial process will be a deductive or an inductive one. Finally, you'll consider opportunities for connecting and sharing your work with others, some potential unintended consequences of those choices, and then, alternative approaches that might mitigate any potential problems. While you may not arrive at hard and fast decisions about your project by the time you've completed this chapter, the self-assessment can help you begin and then continue shaping your plans as you read.

Know that the choices that you make here will help you find your footing, but false starts are common, especially if you're new to this work. As you begin again and then start gaining traction, your purposes will shape-shift. You might find yourself shortening or extending a study, and you will likely need to include additional subjects in your work. You'll find yourself refining your questions, and your purposes will become more nuanced. Answers may present themselves, but if you're fortunate, they won't serve to conclude your learning. They'll inspire new beginnings, and you'll return to this text in order to use it differently all over again.

### TLDR (Too Long Didn't Read)

1. Satisfied documentarians typically have a powerful vision for their sustained learning and work that is far greater than any single project. This is a vision they can continue to pursue even when their titles, roles, and the organizations they serve shift.
2. Documentation projects are built around single moments of learning, collections of moments that look more like journeys, or several journeys that comprise a lengthy expedition.
3. As we prepare to begin a new documentation project, we consider whether we're documenting to remember, understand, or better

serve someone or something. We also consider the people, practices, processes, places, and products that we will study. We determine which modes of memory keeping will serve us best, given these intentions.

4. Our positionality matters within the process. Co-constructing our documentation projects with the people we intend to serve, seeking diverse perspectives, and engaging critical friends can help us notice things we might not have otherwise while mitigating bias.

5. Our purposes for documentation shift over time, and we grow from the process as well. Becoming a documentarian and sustaining our commitment to this work can help us notice and appreciate aspects of a lifelong career that are difficult to discern in the moment. This is one of the greatest rewards of documentation.

## Let's Reflect

Whether you're reading this book for the first time or returning to it again with different needs and interests, you'll want to begin here—by exploring your greater vision and the purposes for this new documentation project. If you're struggling to understand how to create a powerful vision, think of it like this: If your answers to the questions below are dependent on your current role, situation, or system, you haven't crafted a greater vision just yet. You may have a clear purpose for documenting in a very specific context, and that's important. Your vision is something that serves you regardless of where you work or who you intend to serve, though. It's a purpose that is deeply connected to your teacher identity. It's a reflection and product of it as well.

What do you believe about teaching? About learning? About the learners you serve? How are you living those beliefs? And how are you interrogating them? What do you wonder? How are you chasing those curiosities? How are your efforts fulfilling you? If they aren't, what needs to change?

What are the answers to these questions suggesting about what you might document and how?

Which people, places, processes, practices, or products of learning are you eager to better understand?

**Try This: Just-Right Tools and Invitations**

Choose one or more of these challenges in order to deepen your practice.

**Document and Interpret Moment**

Practice documentation like Kenisha might by slowing a moment down. Stay in it, and notice what you see and hear. Document what learners do and say. Capture their representations of things. Compare this work to what you tried at the end of Chapter 1. What's different?

**Document and Interpret a Journey**

Consider your emerging vision and potential purposes for documentation. Capture a series of at least three adjacent moments within a single day or across several days. Look for patterns and emerging themes as you revisit these data. How might they help you refine your emerging vision and purpose?

**Document and Interpret an Expedition**

Reflect on relevant past experiences that might offer insights ahead of any new documentation project. Explore images, recordings, and artifacts that you've gathered over time. What does revisiting them now reveal about the vision behind your learning or work? What were your purposes in the past? How will they shape your next steps as a documentarian?

# References

Bynoe, K., & Thompson, A. (2023). *The gift of playful learning: A guide for educators*. Shell Education.

Centre for Teaching, Learning and Technology, The University of British Columbia. (n.d.). About Us. Indigenous Initiatives. Retrieved June 28, 2023, from https://indigenousinitiatives.ctlt.ubc.ca/about/

Collins, P. H. (2001). *Black feminist thought: Knowledge, consciousness, and the politics of empowerment*. Routledge.

Crenshaw, K. (2017). *On intersectionality: Essential writings*. The New Press.

Duarte, M. E. (2017). *Network sovereignty: Building the internet across Indian country*. University of Washington Press.

Freire, P. (1972). *Pedagogy of the oppressed*. Penguin Education.

Freire, P. (1974). *Education for critical consciousness*. Sheed and Ward.

Latz, A. O. (2017). *Photovoice research in education and beyond: A practical guide from theory to exhibition*. Routledge, Taylor & Francis Group.

Macrorie, K. (1988). *The i-search paper: Revised edition*. Heinemann.

Meyers, S. (2005). *Twilight*. Little and Brown.

Misawa, M. (2010). Queer race pedagogy for educators in higher education: Dealing with power dynamics and positionality of LGBTQ students of color. *International Journal of Critical Pedagogy*, 3(1), 26–35. http://libjournal.uncg.edu/ijcp/article/view/68

Spiegel, C. (2023). *Microjoys: The revolutionary act of uncovering joy when life is not ok*. Piatkus Books.

Vance, J. (2022). *Leading with a Lens of inquiry: Cultivating conditions for curiosity and empowering agency*. Elevate Books.

# 3

# How Will You Use This Book?

As I mentioned previously, this book is not necessarily intended to be read cover-to-cover. Sure, you can move through it that way if you're reading for the first time, and especially if you're new to documenting learning and interested in getting a complete lay of the land. Even so, I recommend skimming it, though—get a sense of this new world, where you might fit within it right now, and how you'd like to traverse it for the very first time. I'm here to shine light down a few promising paths, provide a trusty toolkit for your documentation adventures, and offer fuel for the road. While much of that will come in the form of invitations to try certain approaches or questions worth chewing on, you'll also meet other documentarians along the way—friends in the field whose perspectives are informed by first-hand experiences and sometimes plans that didn't unfold quite the way they expected them to. Some of our best learning is unexpected, and it often makes sense to take the detour, no matter how well we've planned our trip.

*"I've messed up so many advisories by trying to force community," Aaron reflected the last time we spoke, and that got us talking about something that documentation taught both of us quite unexpectedly: When we're patient and take care to put learners in community together, they build community together. They don't really need our help. Often, what they need is for us to get out of the way. Documentation makes us feel better about stepping back, too.*

DOI: 10.4324/9781003333241-5

*"Documentation begets transparency," Aaron said, and I nodded, connecting my teacherly need for quality control to that particular reflection. But that's not what he was getting at really—not at all. "Transparency begets trust, and trust allows for student agency," he continued. "We all just want to feel some sense of belonging, and documentation does that—especially when it's shared. We feel seen."*

And suddenly I'm remembering one sleepy winter morning in 2023 when my students dragged themselves into my Assessment Methods class under a winter storm watch. We were digging into quality rubric design, and I was using a jigsaw approach to decenter myself and study the way they were engaging.

Initially created to disrupt racial bias in schools and better art instruction, John Hattie distinguishes this method as the one having the highest effect size among those studied in his meta-analyses (Hattie, 2023, p. 387). In my experience, it's a necessary component of learning environments that nurture documentation cultures because it invites visible thinking, equitable meaning-making, and learning experiences that de-center teachers in ways that free them up to investigate, capture, and study the effect of their instruction on learning outcomes.

Here's how that worked in my own classroom during last spring:

◆ My students were learning about quality rubric design and wrestling with common criticisms that many make about these tools. Each previewed the Quality Rubrics Wiki (Borgioli Binis, 2016) independently, making note of what they agreed with, what they would argue, where their own experiences with rubric design aligned, and what they would aspire to as teachers once they were leading a classroom of their own. They also captured things they were struggling to understand. This protocol, adapted from one designed by Judith Gray (2005), makes learner's thinking about a text visible.

◆ Next, learners met in home groups of four to share this thinking in rounds. For instance, all learners shared what they agreed with first: one speaker and one point at a time. This continued until all reflections from the text were shared. Then, the group worked to clarify points of confusion before arriving at a determination about the questions that remained.

◆ Each member of the home group was assigned a letter (A–D). Group members then moved into a new group composed of classmates who were also assigned the same letter in their home group. They worked together in these new jigsaw groups to deepen their understanding of rubrics by referencing the wiki they explored, problem-solving around the questions that remained, and connecting concepts together and contextualizing them.

◆ Students returned to their original groups with better and more nuanced understandings. Each home group built a panel for a learning wall that reflected these new understandings. Then, they began using the content on the wall to further connect and question ideas. Additional content was added to the wall in the form of quotes from subject-matter experts in the field, visuals that represented the complexities in the ideas we were exploring, and the intentional use of color.

◆ We used what we learned from this experience and the wall itself to co-create the rubric for our final project. Each learner created a video essay that tackled a specific assessment problem and posed a potential solution. You can read more about this in the case study I've left inside of my digital documentation notebook.

As learners moved in and out of their jigsaw groups, acquiring, connecting, and transferring knowledge from one context to another, I walked the room watching, listening, and documenting my learning.

What surprised me most was how they encouraged one another. I'd challenged them to draw a bit and to rely on their design skills as heavily as their reading comprehension and writing skills to represent and communicate their findings. This was uncomfortable work, and they weren't completely at home with one another yet, either.

Or so I'd thought.

I was touched by how courageous and also—self-deprecating—they were. I was moved by their kindness toward one another and also by the critical lenses they brought to each other's work. They were laughing with one another, asking such good questions, and pausing in all of the right places to wonder a bit, think about things, and then say more.

They didn't need me.

As a young writing teacher, I remember being pleasantly surprised by an unintended benefit of coaching my students to provide quality feedback to one another: It helped them turn toward one another instead of depending entirely upon me for that kind of support, and that allowed me to spend more time with fewer numbers of writers, offer a mid-workshop mini-lesson, or reflect on my own teaching in process. Bringing jigsaw into my classroom at the same time had a similar effect. It was a core practice when I co-taught an inclusive eighth-grade English Language Arts class with my friend, special education teacher Kristen Marchiole early in my career. It remains a powerful protocol in the higher education classes I facilitate today. I use it to teach primary and elementary level writers in my studio and in the classrooms I coach in, too.

When we use jigsaw, students rely on one another more, and this offers us more time to document our learning, ask students good questions that deepen it, and consider the impact of our instructional plans and our teaching. Here, we might also invite others to document beside us as well. We could ask colleagues to donate their time and talent, identify classroom documentarians who assume those roles for a day, a week, or more, or even invite parents or other community members to play a more active role in our classroom experiences. As groups are meeting, we can use bits of this time to side-bar, reflect together, and make meaning from all we are seeing and hearing, as the lesson unfolds. To learn more about this experience and have a peek into how I documented my learning throughout, visit my digital documentation notebook.

There are a few thoughts that I wish experienced documentarians had shared with me when I was a beginner, and I'll sprinkle them throughout this book for your consideration. For instance, while it's true that documentation is an assessment method, it's also true that assessment is far more human than most educators have been trained to believe. Assessment is not synonymous with testing, and in fact, documentation invites us to verb that word whenever possible. Whenever we gather and analyze information in any context, we're making an assessment. Whenever we pay close attention in order to draw conclusions that inform even the slightest decision-making, we're making an assessment. While we might assess to measure a learner's progress toward academic expectations, standards, or objectives, we also make personal and professional assessments all day, every day, whether we're aware of it or not. And while machines and algorithms can assist in many assessment processes, it's ultimately people who determine what's worthy of assessing. It's people who make the judgments and interpret and respond to the results of any assessment, too.

## Assessment Is a Human Endeavor

Every assessment is influenced by a variety of human perspectives, experiences, and values. Assessments are shaped by countless variables, including verbal and nonverbal cues, social and cultural contexts, and personal and emotional factors. Assessment requires empathy and understanding, as humans must consider the unique circumstances and experiences of the individuals or entities being assessed. For instance, when we assess within the context of school, we consider students' diverse identities, strengths, needs, and interests in our attempts to serve them well.

As humans, we also have the ability to reflect on our biases and assumptions. We can consider the limitations of our own knowledge and experience, seek out additional information or perspectives, and revise our assessment plans as needed. So while it's easy to equate assessment as another methodology that helps us measure and report on progress toward academic learning outcomes, experienced documentarians recognize assessment as a uniquely human endeavor that's woven into all that we do to survive and thrive—within and well beyond school. They know that assessment demands a range of cognitive and emotional dispositions, including empathy, curiosity, open-mindedness, persistence, flexibility, reflection, and humility. More importantly, experienced documentarians know that assessment also invites us to interrogate our assumptions, notice our biases, and shift our perspectives.

This is the first thing that I wish I had known when I was a beginner: Assessment is so much more than defining and remediating perceived deficits—in any context. In fact, experience has taught me that when I use documentation to merely mind and attempt to mend gaps, documenting learning is rarely as productive or rewarding as it needs to be in order to serve me or my students well. That said, documentation can mitigate the harm done by over-testing and relying on worksheets or similar tools to assess progress toward learning outcomes. If this is your purpose for reading, know that I will take care to satisfy this need. I do hope that you carry much more away from this text, though. I hope you leave inspired to document for purposes you never imagined, and I hope that effort changes deepen your relationship with your students, yourself, and teaching, too.

Documenting my learning about assessment has been quite an expedition, and I unpack pieces of it for you in my documentation notebook. Here's the short story, though: I used to think that assessment was a practice that enabled me to come to understand learners better. As I began to learn more about the importance of multimodal expression and the role it can and should play within the assessment arena, my thinking about this became more nuanced. I realized, for instance, that if I was truly interested in understanding learners better, it would be important for me to interrogate print privilege and understand how demanding the use of written words when assessing mastery of content and skills that have little to do with them is inequitable and, in fact, doing great harm. Now, my thinking has shifted again.

Documentation has taught me that when I invite learners to demonstrate progress toward outcomes using multimodal expression and then invite them to transition these ideas to written words, I'm confronted with all that I don't know or understand just yet. I also find my own biases revealed to me. I'm changed by this, and that matters. Perhaps this is what assessment can become: An experience that enables students and teachers to grow and evolve together. Perhaps the shifts we make together won't be in practice, process, or performance alone. Assessment might change our attitudes, beliefs, values, and the cultures we create, too.

*"As we think about honoring learning processes, we need to remember that learning extends beyond the classroom too," Kenisha reminds me. "Sometimes, we don't recognize this: Learning moves beyond our classroom walls." Kenisha and Angelique have invited parents to bring artifacts of learning that happened at home into school, where their discoveries can be honored and where teachers might learn from them, too.*

*"Documentation is a bridge," Kenisha explains. "It connects what we do at school to what happens at home, and what happens at home should inform what we do at school."*

*Parents can become partners in this work. How they look at their children's work and how they listen will be different from the observations teachers make, and this is a wonderful thing. It can help everyone learn more, in service to children. It can help everyone become more reflective and even more enthusiastic about learning, too. Including their own.*

## Documentation Is Inductive and Deductive

When I was a new documentarian, my process was mostly deductive: I documented in order to test the best practices I'd culled from my professional learning. Often, those practices were situated as potential solutions to perceived problems I'd identified with my own teaching, how my students were learning, or what they were producing as a result. I began with a dilemma and a theory that experts deemed useful, carrying both into my classroom beside a plan that defined what I would document as I implemented this practice, when I would document, and how. And I still do this sometimes, especially when I'm working with teachers who are striving to improve student learning outcomes by implementing research-based best practices. Still, that beginning typically inspires a more inductive process—one that aims to help me formulate a theory based upon all of that I've learned from the documentation experience itself. Much of that learning is unintentional and unexpected, but time and again, I find that this is where the most satisfying discoveries are made.

Here's what's interesting about that and another thing I wish I'd known when I was a beginner: False starts aren't failures, and they aren't always an indication that I'm ill-prepared to do good work. Often, they're simply a signal that my deductive approach isn't working. Shifting to an inductive posture often helps me gain traction as a learner. I hope that this suggestion serves you well in your beginnings, too: When things feel like they're going off the rails, don't quit. Shift your approach. When we shift how we learn, what we learn often becomes far more satisfying.

## Prioritizing Your Learning and Your Relationships with Learners

It's almost impossible to document and teach well at the same time unless teachers are partnered with dedicated documentarians whose jobs are devoted to capturing learning.

We'll explore methods for managing these far less than ideal realities shortly, but for now, I simply want to offer an uncommon bit of permission: Protect your learning and your relationships with your students. Stay present. See and ensure that your students feel seen as well. Documentation is important, but too often, we disrupt a meaningful moment by pausing to pull out our phones or asking learners to repeat something brilliant so that we might capture it. Sometimes, this isn't a problem, but I find that it's more important for me to remain present and immersed in the moment than it is for me to perfectly document it. Interrupting a student who is revealing something important about their learning might improve the quality of the data that I gather, but at what cost? No one should be treated like a subject inside of an experiment. Documentation is a way of being, it isn't a transaction.

Remaining present also protects my own learning. When I reach for my phone or start scribbling on a clipboard or pad, observation and listening is undermined by my need to multitask. No longer a focused observer or listener who is engaged with those around me, I turn inward to reflect and make meaning from what happened moments prior, instead. Sometimes, this makes good sense, but sometimes, I feel much like I do when someone starts processing a movie while we're still in the theater and the actors are still moving across the screen. It's hard to watch a film and analyze it at the same time.

*When I shared my thoughts about adjacent moments with Klara in June of 2023, she began nodding vigorously on her side of the Zoom screen.*

*"In our Learning Commons, you know, we only have a certain amount of time," she sighed regretfully. "We're really pressured to get things finished. So, we take a lot of pictures of their work, but then classroom teachers go back the next day and sit with those students one-on-one and ask good questions that help all of us understand more about what was happening in and around the moment that we captured the day before."*

*I wonder how you might enlist helpers in your work. How might other teachers, assistants, and even volunteers become partners in your documentation projects? And how might you accept—like so many of my documentarian friends do—the constraints and limitations within your own particular context? Rather than fighting against them, how might you work within them?*

*My own documentation work has improved slowly but dramatically over the years, as I've found good helpers of my own. I've learned to ask students to become documentarians beside me, even when the entire class may not yet be documenting their learning consistently. I've invited parents to document beside me in different settings as well, and most importantly, I've asked colleagues to do the same. This actually transformed the way that I approach coaching work in the systems that I serve, and I find that it balances the power dynamics inside of instructional coaching relationships in important ways. Coaches are not experts. They're learners, and when they position themselves this way and invite the teachers they serve to help them grow, it reinforces this notion. When I'm willing to be an authentic and even vulnerable teacher, this gives others permission to do the same. I find that this, more than any expertise that I might share, enriches learning cultures.*

This is why I find that, depending on my purposes, sometimes it's perfectly okay if I don't document THE moment as it's happening. Often, the most meaningful learning moments are often unexpected and fleeting anyway. It's hard to plan for their arrival, let alone snap the right picture or record the best summaries of what I just heard or observed. I can't tell you how many times

I failed to document THE moment but instead, captured a moment that was adjacent to THE moment, and because I chose to remain present, the memories of THE moment are powerful enough to expand and then rough-in the frame. I used to tell myself that this was enough—the capturing of adjacent moments—and when I did, I employed a somewhat apologetic tone, as if I'd failed to get it right. Now I know that documenting adjacent moments is often ideal. My commitment to remaining present creates longer learning moments and stronger memories. Ultimately, the questions, ideas, and discoveries I make tend to be better for it.

> Would you like to talk shop a bit? I'm easy to find on social media. Search for @AngelaStockman on LinkedIn and I'm @Angela_MakeWriting on Instagram. I'd love to learn from you.

## Approaching Documentation as a Way of Being

Documentation taught me every true thing that I know about teaching and learning, and that learning hasn't always been comfortable or easy—especially when the stakes were high, I felt responsible for delivering simple answers, or time was very tight.

If I'm being honest, documentation has often left me feeling alone in my work and disinvited from certain professional circles, too. For instance, documentation taught me to interrogate everything I thought I knew about teaching writing well. It also helped me understand that a practice is only best if I know how to replicate it in ways that actually serve me or my students well. This humbled me. It still humbles me. At times, it also leaves me confused. When I'm feeling this way now, I try to be patient in my practice, slow to judge, and careful not to assume. I wish I'd known when I was a beginner that the small certainties shaped by a single documented moment often unravel as greater journeys unfold. And each journey is just one small leg of each sustained expedition that typically complicates my thinking and the theories I've created along the way. Documentation has made me less certain, which has made me a more effective and useful teacher. It's made me a terrible trainer but a far better professional learning facilitator, too.

I no longer set out with something to prove as a documentarian. I document to learn, and even as the observations I make and the data I gather validate what I think I know, they almost always reveal the cracks in every foundation I pour and the gaps in every story I try to tell myself about learners and learning. You might wonder then, why anyone would bother to do this at all. Answers are important, and I understand the urgency to chase them. They're often illusory, though. They also breed a false confidence that can do great harm, not only to children but also to teachers and the profession as a whole. What documentation fails to provide in terms of answers it delivers tenfold when it comes to deepening our expertise, our relationships with one another, our classroom culture, and our abilities to understand and advocate for ourselves.

This is slower work that feels less sure, and I imagine this is why few commit to approaching documentation as a way of being. My closest documentation companions are teachers who have been around a block or two and who have had their own certainties rocked hard. They document because they're committed to their learning, and they're committed to their learning because they know how impossible it is to demand answers from a field that is still in its infancy and built on a bedrock of bias.

When I began to embrace documentation as a way of being, I became more gentle with myself as a documentarian. I accepted that I would capture many moments that I didn't have time to process and that there would be days, weeks, and entire chunks of years where any number of other demands on my time and energy prevented me from documenting consistently or even at all. I accepted the fact that even when I did take care to document a moment or a journey well, I wouldn't always have the background knowledge or awareness needed to draw meaningful conclusions from the work. Documenting my learning would help me understand where my own learning was incomplete, where confusions existed, and the work that awaited me—the work that was not yet done.

As I prepared to write this book, I found myself revisiting thousands of photos, videos, and annotations. I revisited dozens of notebooks and reopened countless learning stories that seemed to end without a satisfying resolution. I notice things now that I could not recognize then. I've learned more. I've grown. Experience has changed me. This isn't to say that I didn't take plenty away from documenting my learning in the past. I did, but what I want you to know is that embracing documentation as a sustained way of being has offered so much more.

Moments are fleeting, and journeys come to a quick end. I approach documentation as a life-long expedition now. I have no doubt it will sustain me through the whole of my career. I know for certain that I'll remain a teacher and a learner long after I retire, too. I imagine myself sitting in a rocking chair somewhere in the future, flipping through photos, listening to the voices of the teachers and the students I served, and noticing—again and always— things that I do not right now, even as I have the audacity to write a book

*Figure 3.1—Common Documentation Challenges and Potential Solutions*

about all that I think I know about documentation. It isn't much, but I hope it's just enough. This is what I want for you. No matter your plans, I hope that the encouragement I offer in Figure 3.1 offers useful perspective from the outset of your journey. I hope it helps you regain it if you need to in the future, too.

## What's Your Vision?

I began this chapter by suggesting that you skim the contents of this book before you begin thinking about how you might use it. I'm ending it with an invitation to choose and begin planning your own project. How will you use this book? How will you document in order to remember, understand, or serve something or someone a bit better? Will this new project challenge you to document a moment or a journey, or are you embarking on a sustained expedition?

In Chapter 2, I introduced the Documentation Kaleidoscope, a tool that helps us define our purposes without constricting them.

Come find me on social media if you'd like a companion in the work. I'd love to know more about your plans, help you troubleshoot, and keep you company along the way.

## TLDR (Too Long, Didn't Read)

1. Documentation is all about assessment, but assessment and testing are not synonymous. Documentation and assessment are treated as verbs within this text and as very human endeavors that are shaped by personal, cultural, social, and emotional contexts. Both experiences evolve us. They change our attitudes, values, beliefs, and the cultures we co-create with students.

2. Deductive documentation approaches make a study of existing theories. Inductive documentation approaches aim to develop theories from the documentation experience. Often, false starts or dissatisfying documentation efforts become more productive when we shift our stance from inductive to deductive or from deductive to inductive.

3. When we approach documentation as a way of being rather than a task we complete in order to repair people or things we assume to be broken, we're better able to prioritize our learning, cultivate closer relationships with those we serve, deepen our self-awareness, and hone our expertise.

4. Moments are fleeting, and our presence beside learners is everything. Sometimes, we're unable to capture THE moment. Capture adjacent moments instead. Return to reflect afterward. Work as well as you can within the constraints of your particular context. This is messy and uncertain work. The moment that seems meaningless today may become a piece of a powerful future expedition.

## Let's Reflect

If you've already begun documenting your learning, assess your satisfaction levels and then ask yourself: Is my process mostly inductive or deductive, and how might that be contributing to the way you feel about it? If you have not yet begun, consider which of those approaches might serve you best. How might shifting your posture change the experience?

**Try This: Just Right Tools and Invitations**

**Document and Interpret a Moment**

Practice deductive documentation. Identify a best practice that you'd like to test in your own classroom, and document what you learn about how it serves your students within a single moment. Use the Documentation Kaleidoscope to guide your planning, and use the preceding reflection questions to sink further into your analysis.

**Document and Interpret a Journey**

Document what you learn about how a best practice serves your students within a single moment. Then, interpret those findings. Determine which postures will serve you best as you take your next steps. Document at least two additional learning moments. Notice whether the whole of your study was mostly inductive or deductive. How might a different posture have changed your experience and findings?

**Document and Interpret an Expedition**

Identify one best practice that has had longevity in your classroom. Locate evidence of its presence at different points in time. Was your confidence in its efficacy driven by inductive or deductive assessment processes? What questions arise now, after you've read this chapter?

## References

Borgioli Binis, J. (2016, September). How do we define quality rubrics? Retrieved July 2023. http://qualityrubrics.pbworks.com/w/page/992395/Home

Gray, J. (2005). *Four "A"s text protocol*. National School Reform Faculty.

Hattie, J. (2023). *Visible learning: The sequel*. Taylor & Francis.

# Part II

# Planning Your Own Documentation Project

# 4

# Will You Document a Moment, a Journey, or a Lengthy Expedition?

When we think about planning in nearly any context, we often imagine linear project management tools. We like checklists and bullet journals. We use spreadsheets and outlines. When things get complicated, we begin to lean on flow charts or mind maps. Still: Our plans are orderly, and they intend to make our methodology that way. This isn't a bad thing—planning matters. If we know what we hope to achieve, defining a clear pathway toward that goal makes the journey predictable, efficient, and, no doubt, more rewarding than it would be if we simply laced up our boots and started hiking into the unknown without a compass or a guide. So, that's what this chapter intends to offer you—the tools you will need to plan a documentation project. Here's the thing, though: Most documentation projects don't unfold in a linear fashion.

Remember the Documentation Kaleidoscope I placed in your hands as you were reading Chapter 2? Let's play with it a bit. Hold it up to the light of your own learning landscape, and begin turning it a bit. Notice each tile that frames your vision and, more importantly, how they tumble for you. Try to be conscious of the experiences and expertise you're bringing to this experiment, as well. Remember that when you make observations through the kaleidoscope, what you see is a bit other-worldly. The kaleidoscope helps you recognize just how multifaceted and complex learners and learning can be.

Here's something you should know: Kaleidoscopes work by reflecting light. And while light travels in a straight line, it quickly changes direction whenever it bumps into something. This is what I notice in the classroom when I begin chasing light, and maybe you do, too. Light bounces, and those kaleidoscope tiles tilt and slip as each learning moment unfolds. The mosaic

DOI: 10.4324/9781003333241-7

is never arranged the same way twice. Experienced documentarians know that this is what makes the work so meaningful and so different from classic assessment and research methods. It's one of the reasons they value it. If you're new to this work, you might quickly become overwhelmed by this reality, though. Previous practice has taught us to steady our assessments inside of static tools like tests, essays, and even projects that we can collect and grade. If this is your world, know that any discomfort you feel as you begin documenting your learning is not uncommon. There will be times when it seems as though you're losing your way. Know that you're not. Learning is messy, right? Documenting it can be, too.

*Klara documents her learning because many of the students she serves in Mississauga, Ontario, are refugees who are new English learners. There are 35 different languages spoken in their school, where children arrive from war-torn countries with families who are weary with a sort of relief that no human being should ever have to endure.*

*"My parents came here because I wasn't allowed to have books in Afghanistan," one of her students recently told her. "They wanted me to read and go to school." And so they left the only home they ever knew.*

*Minutes fly by in the Learning Commons where Klara is a teacher-librarian and experienced documentarian who takes care to co-create her learning experiences with students, gather critical friends, and maintain a deep awareness of her own biases.*

*The light bounces in many directions around Klara whenever she brings young makers and writers together. They have important stories to tell, but she knows that if she rushes them to print, they'll fall silent. So, she offered them loose parts—materials like buttons, blocks, and clay—and invited them to build their understanding of the word lovely.*

*"This was so eye-opening," she said. "Their happiness. Their joy. How they interpreted the word 'lovely' and used loose parts to represent it—it helped me learn so much about them and where they came from. If I'd expected them to write, they wouldn't have been able to communicate their ideas."*

*Klara invited learners to build their experiences with anger, too. And she was just as humbled and enlightened by the results. As storymaking began, Klara found—like I so often do—that structure was an important constraint. Learners knew that they could represent the beginning, middle, and end of their story in any way they wished, pulling on different modes of expression and relying on documentation to contain the products that emerged from the process.*

*"What were your purposes for documentation?" I asked, and Klara told me that she needed to learn more about how these writers were conceptualizing a story. They arrived from such very different places, and their understanding of what stories are and how they are constructed was very different. Inviting loose parts to play, experimenting with story structure, and documenting what she saw and heard helped her understand her students' strengths, background knowledge, and interests, too. They shifted her understanding of how stories were created and made.*

*Documentation set the tiles in her own kaleidoscope tumbling over and over again as she moved these writers from idea generation to story composition and then to the creation of stop-motion videos, animated short films, and multimedia story books. You can follow this journey from start to finish by dipping into my digital documentation notebook if you wish.*

*What struck me most about Klara's interpretation of this experience followed shortly after our interview concluded, when she messaged me on Twitter to quickly follow up.*

*"Thanks for chatting with me the other night," she wrote. "I'm doing a lot of work and continuing to learn about Indigenous ways of knowing and being and two-eyed seeing. I have learned so much, but I know that there is so much more to learn as well. After our chat, I thought about our colonial view of pedagogical documentation—and what might need to change in the process. If we were to look at it from an Indigenous worldview, how might that change our understanding of what it is and what it could be?"*

*These questions have stayed with me, and I wonder: What are your thoughts and experiences here? Are you willing to share? You'll find Klara (@kindyfriends) and me (@AngelaStockman) on Twitter. We'd love to learn from you.*

Learning is unpredictable, and learners become our teachers. It always gets messy. So let's plan for that. Let's plan to have your plan disrupted. Let's plan for knots in the process, side-trips, and detours. Let's plan to feel a bit disoriented, and let's make sure you're equipped with tools that can help you find your footing and a just-right path for each leg of your documentation journey.

Remember that kaleidoscopes are toys, not games. This may seem like a silly distinction, but I find it's an important one. Toys are designed for individual, imaginative play that stimulates open-ended and divergent thinking.

Games, on the other hand, are typically designed for multiple participants. Built around structured rules, competition, and achieving specific objectives, games are all about strategy, performance, victory, and defeat. Documentation protocols and best practices exist to bring a game-like structure and satisfaction to your learning and work, but they shift in response to your interests and needs. You won't be rushing to a finish line here, competing with yourself, or seeking to best anyone else. There are no rules. I can appreciate the need for a good playbook, though. So that's how you should treat the second part of this book—beginning with this chapter.

## Using Part Two Like a Playbook

Playbooks provide guidance, strategies, resources, and tools for specific activities or endeavors. Ours happens to be documentation. While the first part of this book acquainted you with the concept and invited you to begin defining your own relationship with it, this second part will equip you for the road and serve as a travel guide along the way. Here, you'll find structures, protocols, and techniques that will serve your own documentation project well. If you're longing for step-by-step instructions, I'll leave them here for you beside examples, peeks into my own practice, and connections to friends in the field whose own experiences with documentation might inspire you. Look for these signposts along the way:

◆ **Kaleidoscope:** Any time you see the kaleidoscope, look for a use case that demonstrates how a specific documentarian studied learning in a particular context and the steps that you might take in order to do the same.

◆ **Flashlight:** As your guide, I'll take care to shine a bit of light on aspects of this work that you may not be inclined to notice. Each time you see the flashlight, look for suggestions, tips, and even bits of advice that may enliven, revive, or, if needed—steady—your adventure.

◆ **Question Mark:** Answers to frequently asked questions will be tucked into the margins of this section. You'll find them by following the question mark. Remember to come find me on social media, too. I'd love to talk shop with you! I'm @AngelaStockman on Twitter and @angela_makewriting on Instagram.

◆ **Pencil:** I've left a variety of creative invitations throughout this section of the book. They challenge you to document your learning about the documentation process. Wherever you see the pencil, pause to capture evidence of your learning, doodle, draw, and reflect. Use sticky notes if you'd like, rather than directly marking up the book. This way, when you return in the future, you'll be able to use these prompts again in your new and very different context.

## Clarifying Your Vision

You may already have an outcome for your project in mind, but before you dive in, find the pencil and its related prompts inside of this chapter. Use those questions to consider how you would like documentation to enrich your life. Rather than focusing on a specific project or the distinct purposes or goals that align to it, reflect on what it means to *be* a documentarian and to commit to this practice in a sustained way—perhaps for the whole of your career.

> Let's say that you dedicate the next ten years to documenting your own learning. How will you know if your efforts were worth it? How would you be changed by the process? How would your commitment to documentation have served your students well, too? Keep honing your vision and thinking about the difference that documentation might make in your life over time if you actually had no end-game in mind.

As I prepared to write this book, I dug through decades of documentation work. I've kept tubs full of my notebooks and journals in a storage unit a few miles away from my house. You can peek into those tubs in my digital documentation notebook, too.

I've documented my learning beside students in Google Photos, Google Drive, Seesaw, and Unrulr as well. I've reflected around documentation panels with teachers in dozens of different school districts. I've recorded too many hours of audio and video to count. Revisiting these images, interviews, and artifacts reminded me of how often it felt like I was failing. There were many false starts and abandoned efforts. There were weeks, months, and even an entire year when I didn't document well. I rarely had enough time to reflect as deeply as I wanted to in any of those moments. But then, there were other projects that seemed to take on a life of their own. There were journeys where I felt like I was simply along for a ride that would teach me much, as long as I kept my sticky fingers off of the controls. And from my current vantage point, years after I began documenting my learning, I can see how each moment and journey was a ripple that built the wave I'm riding as I write this book for you. Those ripples mattered, but this wave was career-changing and even life-changing. Documentation has kept me hopeful, captivated by learners and learning, and better able to see the forest for the trees. There have been incredible challenges, unfair, and, at times, even unacceptable circumstances to endure and walk away from entirely over my last thirty years as an educator. There were learners I was able to serve well, and there were too many that I worry I failed. Sometimes, when I look back at a moment or a journey I documented long ago, I notice important things that I didn't have an eye or a mind for back then. Teachers are humans. If I've learned anything from my sustained documentation work, it's this. Binary thinking and the rush to quick conclusions are often the stuff of fear or arrogance or both. There is so much happening inside of any learning moment that we aren't able to see, let alone comprehend. They're a reflection of our brilliance, and also, our great limitations.

I didn't have a playbook to work from when I began, and it wasn't until recently that I was able to give shape to the processes I use: The Documentation Kaleidoscope is a good fit. I wonder how it's feeling in your hands, now that you've had a moment to think about your greater vision. Shortly, you'll use it to begin planning a documentation project. For right now, I'd just like you to experiment with it a bit. This tool isn't for planning alone. It's for visioning. Dreaming. Considering opportunities and approaches you may not have considered before. I hope they're becoming clearer to you.

---

✎ It might be helpful to download and print the Documentation Kaleidoscope, assemble it, and manipulate it for a bit. I've left a download in the appendix for just these purposes. Print it, cut each sphere out, layer them together, and fasten them together through the center. Keep things loose enough to allow for easy turning. Spin the kaleidoscope, and let the tiles tumble and settle into different configurations. Connect them to your past experiences. How have you been a documentarian, even unintentionally? Scroll the photo album on your phone. Notice the videos you've captured. Dig into your social media posts—go back as far as you can.

What have you documented? Who have you documented? Why have you documented? What made it matter? Perhaps you didn't realize that you were documenting your learning all along or, at the very least, preparing to. Use the Documentation Kaleidoscope to recognize and define your beginnings. Use it to generate new ideas, too.

Bring the Documentation Kaleidoscope to your work. Use it to notice things about your documentation habits and tendencies that you haven't previously noticed. Use it to get a sense of your interests, needs, and values. Use it to shape your greater vision—the one that will keep you learning far beyond any single moment.

## Documentation Is a Knotty Process

We document small learning moments. We also document learning journeys and entire expeditions. Often, when we commit to one set of purposes, we prepare to document in small or significant ways only to discover that we need to shift our posture and change our plan as we sink into our work. Documenting our learning typically uncovers new purposes. It almost always invites us to revise our initial plans or create entirely new ones.

> When I was an inexperienced documentarian, the process often left me feeling defeated. I'd entered a new project with specific questions, needs, and interests. I didn't necessarily hope for quick answers, but I certainly assumed that all of my hard work would be clarifying. And it usually was—eventually. The process was never simple or linear, though, and the clarity I achieved often blurred theories that I'd once held in sharp relief. It was often complex and recursive. It was also, when I kept the faith, deeply rewarding.

I offer this to reassure you: Documentation is a knotty process. What feels like a false start is often a bit of early, authentic, and important learning. So, follow the questions where they lead you and work with the light you're given. Continue documenting, reflecting, and adjusting your plan as you go. Return to this chapter and the others in the second part of this book whenever you need to reorient yourself. Remember, this is an adventure. The quality of your learning is dependent on your willingness to explore unbeaten paths. Traveling a straight path through this process might be easier—and I certainly encourage you to start there, especially if you're a beginner. Don't be afraid to take the detours that the process offers you, though. Don't assume that each is a dead-end.

> **?** "What if the leaders who support me intended for me to use docu-
> mentation to follow a very specific path for very specific purposes and
> something completely unexpected happens?" you might ask. "What if the
> documentation project doesn't unfold as we assumed it would and we find
> ourselves taking a huge detour that makes them really uncomfortable?"
>    Take the detour.
>    Use what you discover to pose theories about how you might bet-
> ter meet the needs identified by your leaders. Use what you learn to
> suggest uncommon and perhaps—more productive—opportunities or
> solutions.

## Choosing an Inductive or Deductive Approach

I like to plan a new documentation project by thinking about what I hope
to learn from it and whether my initial process will be a deductive one that
aims to test a promising practice or theory that I'm already familiar with or
an inductive one that intends to produce an entirely new and often—unexpected—theories. If you've read *Make Writing: 5 Strategies that Turn Writer's
Workshop into a Makerspace* (Times 10 Publications, 2015), then you should
know that that book was the result of what was initially a deductive documentation project that forced me to take a detour, evolved over the course of
several journeys, became highly inductive, and remains an expedition that
continues to teach me surprising and very important things.

If you've read any of my *other* books, they're each the result of documentation projects that remained far more deductive. I began with theories of
my own or those shaped by other mentors and experts in the field, tested
them, and documented my learning along the way. These were very different
learning—and writing—experiences.

When I reflect on the ways I've approached documentation over the
years, I can see how each experience is always a bit of a waltz, though. My
learning partners and I turn rhythmically—around and around—as we move
through each moment or journey. We shift from inductive to deductive postures and back again, as we notice, capture, reflect, and return our attention
to the learning again.

I find that once I move beyond learning in any single moment, my purposes almost always have to shift a bit in order to continue chasing the light.
For instance, Max taught me much inside of that moment when they began
storymaking with LEGO. As I began paying closer attention and documenting that learning, new questions emerged, and adjacent inquiries were driven

by a more deductive process. As an entire learning expedition began to grow up around that initial learning moment, my approach became even more deductive still. Initial theories were grounded in the evidence that I gathered from my work with young writers. Those that followed were further informed by a close study and synthesis of research conducted by experts in different fields of study. Most of those findings were shared in the books that I wrote after *Make Writing*, especially *Creating Inclusive Writing Environments in the K-12 Classroom: Reluctance, Resistance, and Strategies that Make a Difference* (Stockman, 2021).

Once I have a sense of my vision, my more specific purposes as a documentarian inside of a new project, and whether my initial approach will be inductive or deductive, I'm ready to begin planning my project, keeping in mind that this plan will shapeshift as it unfolds and that this is what makes documentation authentic, meaningful, and, ultimately, satisfying.

The table in Figure 4.1 shows the questions I consider as I prepare to launch a new documentation project. My process was influenced by Joanne Picone-Zocchia, Giselle Martin-Kniep, and Diane Cunningham, founders of Communities for Learning, Leading Lasting Change. Together, they conceptualized the ARCS Framework for sustainable improvement (Kniep, 2008).

## Using the ARCS Framework to Plan a Documentation Project

| Alignment | Representation | Culture | Sustainability |
|---|---|---|---|
| How will I ensure that these purposes align to the greater vision for who I am trying to become?<br><br>How might align my documentation efforts to:<br>• My own interests and needs?<br>• The needs and interests of those I serve?<br>• The needs and interests of the system I serve?<br><br>How will I intentionally assess alignment as I plan and work through this project?<br><br>How will I know when misalignment exists?<br><br>How might I plan to address this? | Whose voices and perspectives should inform the way I plan my project?<br><br>Who should provide perspective as it unfolds? How?<br><br>Who should be involved in the interpretation of the findings?<br><br>How will I ensure that those who will be most affected by this work have significant influence over its design and the way it is executed?<br><br>How will I continue to assess representation as this project unfolds?<br><br>How will I mitigate misrepresentation in my work? | What is my vision of the culture I hope to shape through my teaching, learning, and documentation efforts?<br><br>Which norms, values, protocols, and dispositions will I intentionally cultivate?<br><br>Who might help me better understand the potential consequences of my choices and their impact on community culture?<br><br>How will I engage critical friends and seek diverse perspectives as I plan and execute my project? | How will I sustain the most meaningful aspects of this work beyond the present moment?<br><br>How will this learning, in this moment, for these very specific purposes nurture and sustain my greater vision?<br><br>When I look back on this project in the distant future, how will I remember it in the context of the greater legacy that I hope to leave behind?<br><br>Who might sustain this thinking, learning, or work in my absence? How do I make all of this accessible to them right now? How do I position myself as a partner in this learning? |

*Figure 4.1—Using the ARCS Framework to Plan a Documentation Project*

Consisting of four elements—alignment, representation, culture, and sustainability—this framework is one I turn to in many contexts in order to design and improve plans of all kinds. As a documentarian, I treat each of those four elements as lenses through which I view the landscape I intend to document within, the people I will attempt to learn about and from, and the processes, practices, and products of learning that emerge from each moment, journey, or expedition.

When documentation was new to me, I was privileged to share my early thinking and work with the late Silvia Rosenthal Tolisano. She began blogging about her own experiences and ideas about documentation around the same time that I started sharing my own work, and I deeply appreciated her invitations to collaborate, reflect, and better our beginnings way back then. The best of Silvia's thinking was captured in a book that she co-authored with Janet Hale. *A Guide to Documenting Learning: Making Thinking Visible, Meaningful, Shareable, and Amplified* (Tolisano & Hale, 2018) remains a seminal text for western documentarians and especially those compelled by the heutagogical—or learner-centered—power of documentation. My book is a bit different. It focuses squarely on you—the teacher—and the way that you might become a dedicated documentarian. Still, I can't help but push you toward Silvia and Janet's beautiful book if you haven't read it already. This contribution to the field is immeasurable, and Silvia's legacy lives on in my own learning, too. I hope she continues to inspire you.

## Preparing to Document Your Learning

Remember this, as you prepare to document: Kaleidoscopes only work if we hold them up to the light, and while light travels in a straight line, it changes direction when it bumps into anything. You will have to recalibrate your plan, and this isn't failure. Use the Documentation Kaleidoscope to make—and shift—your purposes, practices, and tools.

Here are a few things to consider, whether you intend to document a moment, a journey, or an expedition:

◆ **Plan to make thinking visible in a moment and learning visible over time, as journeys or expeditions unfold.** Clarifying your vision and articulating a meaningful purpose for your documentation project is helpful here, regardless of your chosen approach. These efforts will deepen your self-awareness, help you define what will serve as meaningful evidence of learning in either context, and notice it when it's happening—especially when you weren't expecting it to.

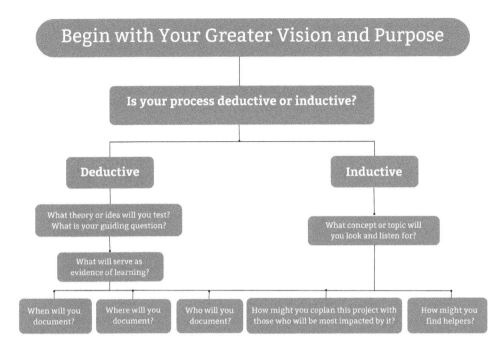

*Figure 4.2—Inductive vs. Deductive Approaches*

As Figure 4.2 suggests, if your process is a deductive one, you will want to define a guiding question or specific learning focus to pursue before you think about the environments and moments that you might document within. It's important to consider what will serve as evidence of learning in your particular context as well and what you will need to look for in order to notice it happening (Tolisano & Hale, 2018, pp. 89–90). If your process is an inductive one, you might begin with a looser concept or topic, instead. You can also enter the learning environment without any preconceived questions or concepts in mind. Some find it overwhelming to document widely and seemingly without purpose, but I'll be honest: This is how much of my documentation work unfolds.

Beginning your work with a clear vision of the ways in which you want documentation to serve you will also help you shift postures when needed. When Max began storymaking with their LEGO, I wasn't intending to document what he was teaching me. Still, I was attuned to my greater vision as a writing teacher and especially sensitive to the presence of resistance in my workshops and studios. When Max conquered their resistance right in front of me, my eyes widened with recognition. My kaleidoscope wasn't in hand at that moment, but it set the tiles in my tumbling, nonetheless. There was no way that I could predict this moment happening, but having a vision and being guided by a greater purpose made me more alert. It made me a more vigilant and reflective practitioner in every context. And that kaleidoscope is always in my proverbial pocket—in close reach. It's a constant companion and a reliable tool that's become a seamless part of my planning and my daily work.

◆ **Plan to capture the learning.** I explore this further in Chapter 6. Determine when and where the learning might happen. Think about who will be involved, and then consider the modes through which they will express themselves. This will help you choose the best methods and tools for your work. For instance, whenever I facilitate a Make Writing Studio session, I know that the first firestarter that I offer on the very first day reveals much about who the writers in the room might be, how they prefer to make and write, and where their individual strengths are. I always take care to document how learners respond in this very specific moment. I'm thoughtful about what I will ask them to do, how I will ask them to represent their writing ideas, and how I will invite them to reflect. Then, I choose my documentation tools accordingly. In my world, photographs and video recordings often allow me to capture the best evidence of learning in that particular context. Figure 4.3 will allow you to make thoughtful choices, too.

◆ **Plan to invite helpers.** It's difficult to teach and document at the same time, and you don't have to go it alone. Who could help you document your learning well? Is it possible to invite a colleague in for the day? Could your students document beside you for specific purposes that help you meet your learning goals? What if you tapped just one or two of them to be documentarians for the day? What if you invited them to document their own learning and relied on their efforts to inform your own? The third part of this book attends to both of those priorities.

◆ **Plan to revise or even scrap the plan.** As you begin to imagine how this learning experience will unfold, consider sketching up a journey map like the one you see in Figure 4.4. This will help you anticipate where your documentation project might gain traction, experience turbulence, take a bit of detour, or fall completely off the rails. You can use your journey map to plan the specific moments you will document. You might also use it to think about where you might slow instruction in order to teach or document well. Journey maps do not need to reflect every move you might make through a learning or documentation experience. Use it to define and reflect on the high

# Modes, Tools, Purposes

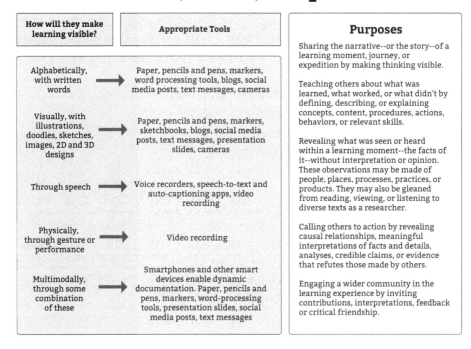

| How will they make learning visible? | Appropriate Tools | Purposes |
|---|---|---|
| Alphabetically, with written words | Paper, pencils and pens, markers, word processing tools, blogs, social media posts, text messages, cameras | Sharing the narrative--or the story--of a learning moment, journey, or expedition by making thinking visible. |
| Visually, with illustrations, doodles, sketches, images, 2D and 3D designs | Paper, pencils and pens, markers, sketchbooks, blogs, social media posts, text messages, presentation slides, cameras | Teaching others about what was learned, what worked, or what didn't by defining, describing, or explaining concepts, content, procedures, actions, behaviors, or relevant skills. |
| Through speech | Voice recorders, speech-to-text and auto-captioning apps, video recording | Revealing what was seen or heard within a learning moment--the facts of it--without interpretation or opinion. These observations may be made of people, places, processes, practices, or products. They may also be gleaned from reading, viewing, or listening to diverse texts as a researcher. |
| Physically, through gesture or performance | Video recording | Calling others to action by revealing causal relationships, meaningful interpretations of facts and details, analyses, credible claims, or evidence that refutes those made by others. |
| Multimodally, through some combination of these | Smartphones and other smart devices enable dynamic documentation. Paper, pencils and pens, markers, word-processing tools, presentation slides, social media posts, text messages | Engaging a wider community in the learning experience by inviting contributions, interpretations, feedback or critical friendship. |

*Figure 4.3—Modes, Tools, and Purposes*

# Journey Mapping

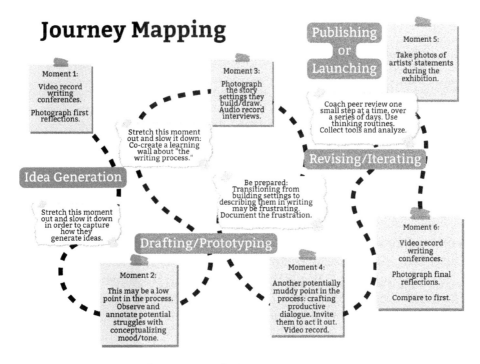

*Figure 4.4—Journey Mapping a Documentation Project*

and low points and how you might respond to the bigger opportunities or challenges. Use it to consider unintended consequences, too. Tinker with the kaleidoscope a bit as you engage in this more strategic and proactive planning. How might you use it to stay engaged in your learning and work as you adjust your plan in process?

*Aaron Schorn reminds me that when we document habitually, we begin to think better on the fly as well. This is a soothing bit of wisdom that I apply during those documentation experiences that feel grossly unproductive.*

*The thing about becoming a documentarian is that the learning that happens is exponential and complex. While we're positioning cameras and pressing record in order to capture the things that we see and hear happening around us, a different and deeper kind of learning is occurring under the surface of that moment.*

*We're becoming attuned to the process. We're learning how to see and hear with greater precision. Our interpretations of each moment are becoming more nuanced. Even our struggles and failures are teaching us things.*

## Planning to Document a Single Moment

As I mentioned earlier, documenting learning often heightens the entire experience. So, it's not uncommon for me to feel a bit angsty as I walk into a classroom or workshop and begin. I know that the minutes will shrink and expand all at once, that sparks might fade faster than my camera can catch them, and that my attention might be pulled in a thousand directions as learners begin teaching me things that I never anticipated.

Remaining grounded in my vision, my purpose, and my guiding questions, concepts, or topics is essential. Creating enough space for documentation matters, too. I typically ask the learners I serve to reflect before, during, and after learning. This is an essential part of quality instruction—it improves their learning outcomes. It also gives me time to document and reflect on my feet, too. Even when I have this kind of time, I still find that I need to give myself grace. Here's why: Sometimes, I'm able to capture the instance that precisely aligns with my preconceived plan. As I mentioned previously though, I often gather photos, recordings, reflections, or artifacts that lived adjacent to the aligned moment instead. As long as I take care to inform this documentation with annotations and my own reflections, the learning isn't compromised. In fact, it's protected by my willingness to remain present, connected, and aware of all that's happening in the moment.

As you might imagine, documenting a single moment is less of a march that demands a sequential procedure than a dance that calls for great choreography instead. I explore this with far greater depth in Chapter 6. Here are some quick planning tips, though:

◆ **Start simply.** Rooting your first documentation experience in a practical and simple study will build your confidence beside your skillset. Start small, and keep it simple. Remember, even the smallest moments have the potential to become journeys, and rewarding journeys inspire whole expeditions. I can't tell you how many times friends in the field dove into complex documentation projects that found them drowning in data and too overwhelmed to sustain their efforts. Simple starts make for lasting learning. They offer a feel for the work, what makes it different from other assessment and reflection endeavors, and how to move through it in a satisfying way. Let the ideas in Figure 4.5 inspire you. Then, consider documenting

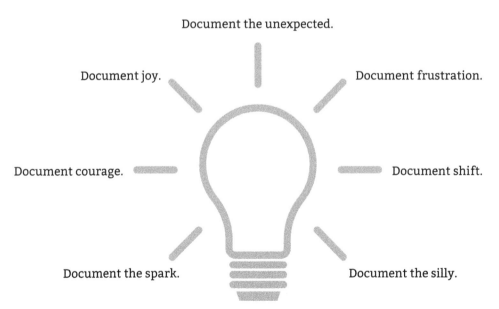

# Simple Ways to Begin

Document the unexpected.

Document joy.

Document frustration.

Document courage.

Document shift.

Document the spark.

Document the silly.

*Figure 4.5—Simple Ways to Begin*

a personal learning moment or journey that has nothing to do with what happens in your classroom first. You might find that this sort of project is precisely what you need in order to reconnect with yourself and grow in rewarding ways. It's not just your teaching that matters—your life matters. How you live it and how you show up for yourself—matters. My friend Kelly Love inspires me here. You'll meet her in my digital documentation notebook.

◆ **Share your intentions from the outset.** Start by sharing your documentation purposes and plans with your students or anyone else who might be involved in the work. Make sure they understand what you will be documenting, how, and why. Take care to tap their perspectives and get clear about their boundaries. Plan to respect them, too. Whenever I'm clear about my plans for documenting learning, students will often approach me with their own perspectives, invitations, and reflections that deepen my work. In this way, transparency matters not only because it's ethical but also because it's rewarding, too. When you tell your students what you're trying to learn and how you're trying to learn it, your students will often show up to teach you things you didn't anticipate, and that's a beautiful thing.

◆ **Invite multimodal expression.** Spoken words are harder to capture than written words, sometimes. What's built is easier to document than the process of building itself. Rapidly prototyping an idea with loose parts might consume far less time than articulating it with written words. Pictures are worth a thousand of those, too. Especially when you record your voice over an image. Hopefully, you thought about all of this prior to documenting your learning, but even in the moment, you'll need to choose and invite the use of multimodal expression intentionally, keeping your goals and the need for efficiency in mind. Many times, the moment will teach you which modes of documentation are best. This is messy stuff, so be prepared for that. It's also something that you will get better at over time. In the meantime, use Figure 4.3 to remain agile in the moment while working within the constraints that challenge you.

◆ **Loosen or tighten your grip.** If you're struggling to gain traction, sustain your momentum, or engage in meaningful documentation work, widen your aperture a bit. Rather than striving to answer a specific question or document evidence of a certain kind of learning, tease out a general concept or capture evidence of where that certain kind of learning could or should have transpired. If your process was already loose, tighten the lens that you're bringing to the work. What questions are emerging as the process is unfolding? Lean into them, and document what you see and hear. If you began with an inductive approach, shift to a deductive stance. If you arrived with certain theories or practices to test, document what you're noticing around them. What's happening behind the scenes, under the cover story of the lesson, or below the surface of the work? If you can't tell, how might you find out?

◆ **Return to the Documentation Kaleidoscope.** Let the tiles tilt and tumble again. If you began by documenting a moment, you might find yourself stretching into a journey or even realizing the potential to begin a full-blown expedition. Notice when your purposes begin to shift. You may start a documentation project with the intention to simply remember or better understand something or someone. As you sink into the work, you may feel pulled in a different direction. Entertain this, and if it compels you, move that way. Try. Similarly, you may find that your plan to document specific people in a particular place or the development of a distinct product isn't as rewarding as you hoped it would be. Use the kaleidoscope to redesign your roadmap. It's the learning that matters inside of this project, not your compliance to any preconceived plan.

*When we test learners using common methods like selected or constructed responses, their answers live within the boundaries of a single page. Documentation invites a sort of assessment that progresses if we let it. It was Silence Karl who reminded me of this shortly after our interview.*

*Silence is a self-taught documentarian who is looking forward to learning more from experts in his field. When we spoke, he had much to say about his intuitive approach to documentation. He credited his mother, Mykal, and others in his homeschooling community for supporting him as he pursued this passion and sharpened his skills so dramatically over time. By the time our interview was over, I'd made a meaningful assessment of how Silence came to be a documentarian, who taught him well, and what he wanted to learn and do next, professionally.*

*It was sometime later when he messaged me with an additional thought, though.*

*"There is one thing I wanted to add at the end of our conversation about my self-taught nature," he wrote. "In a way, a self-taught person is much more privileged than someone with a vocabulary or formal education because education is far easier to obtain*

*than experience or engagement. My experience creates enjoyment because it is controlled by me, and this is a huge advantage as I grow. My experience has been deep because I chose it instead of it being chosen for me."*

*That Silence understood his privilege struck me hard. And that he was able to see his positionality in a way that other 16-year-olds might not be something, too.*

*"Thanks for listening," he said. And I was grateful. As I share this story here and my truth of it, as I know it, I wonder if this was what Silence intended me to take away from the entire experience. I wonder what his interpretation of it all would be if he reflected on this moment, too.*

*This is what documentation enables all of us to do. Assessment isn't testing. It's not best contained within a single moment. It's about seeking understanding, and that often takes time. It's a journey, or more often, an expedition.*

◆ **Invite diverse perspective-taking.** Hale and Tolisano remind us to keep two things in mind as we actively document our learning: Our purpose (why we are documenting) and our perspective (what we plan to say and who we plan to say it to) (Tolisano & Hale, 2018, p. 93). It's important to remain aware of your personal identity and positionality as well. Our purposes and perspectives are dramatically influenced by our histories and experiences, as well our race, abilities, ethnicity, and gender. Who we are influences what—and how—we notice. It influences the conclusions we reach. Our positionality has significant influence within the documentation experience as well. Inviting those who are different from us to document and share their own learning inside the same experience reveals much that might be overlooked otherwise. Actively seeking their perspectives on shared moments can help us interrogate our own, and this matters. You'll find additional strategies to support this work in Chapter 7.

Even when I'm documenting my own learning, I take care to decenter myself in the process as much as possible. I want to hear from the subjects my research intends to serve. I want to elevate their voices instead of my own, and I want to ensure that I'm thinking about those who are not yet represented but must be if my learning is to be complete. You can learn more about how I've acted with intention here by visiting my digital documentation notebook, where several use cases are shared.

## Expanding a Single Moment into a Journey or an Expedition

Often, even when we intend to document just a single learning moment, what happens within that moment inspires a more sustained process. What we see and hear piques new and different curiosities, challenges deeply held beliefs or assumptions, or illuminates gaps in our reasoning, design flaws, or opportunities that are worth chasing. It's not uncommon for our learning to feel incomplete as we wind down our documentation of a single moment, but it can be hard to connect what's learned in one moment to what we will study in another. These tips might help you here:

◆ **Conduct additional observations within a similar context, but shift your purpose, point of view, and practice.** For instance, after Max began making stories with LEGO, I began offering different loose parts and documenting how they and other children made stories with them.

◆ **Analyze these initial moments and identify specific elements that could be explored further.** Returning to Max, their classmates, and their use of varied loose parts, I noticed that many of them chose to build with LEGO or PlayDoh, even when they had access to abundant and very different materials. This inspired me to begin interviewing children about why they chose the materials they did. All of them told me that they preferred making stories with loose parts that were familiar to them. All of them played with blocks, LEGO, PlayDoh, or clay at home, and this experience made them comfortable with creative tools.

◆ **Document each identified key element at work inside of different moments, providing detailed accounts of what was seen and heard.** This is how I began to understand the influence of open-ended materials on idea generation and development: I offered learners an array of materials to work with, I invited them to make stories, and then I documented their processes. I also asked them to tell me their stories, taking note of whether each was complete and getting a sense of how rewarding it was for writers to create stories with materials other than written words. They reflected aloud as I walked the room, and I captured their stories using the Otter.ai app. Its voice-to-text translation is highly reliable, allowing me to notice keyword trends and repeated expressions.

◆ **Make connections across varied moments. Analyze the relationships and connections between the different documented moments.** Look for patterns, themes, or common threads that emerge, as well as potential learning trajectories or progressions. The documentation journey that I describe in this series of examples helped me understand that some loose parts are more open-ended than others and that when writers are struggling to identify or develop ideas, offering a part that is looser or tighter than the one they're working with often helps them gain traction.

◆ **Contextualize your learning.** Consider how each moment relates to previous or future experiences, contributing to your sustained learning and even the pursuit of your greater vision. As a young and inexperienced teacher, I grew discouraged each time I met a writer who presented as resistant. Documenting my learning, the influence of open-ended materials on engagement, idea development, and the quality of resulting written words connected those past experiences to my present learning while inspiring new and interesting questions for me to chase in the future. For example, my documentation work was teaching me that materials mattered in the writing classroom, but I didn't know why, and I was only beginning to see how. Future journeys would offer clarifying clues that deepened and refined my thinking.

◆ **Communicate and share.** Share the expanded moments of pedagogical documentation with your students, the adults in their lives, your colleagues, administrators, and those in your expanded professional network. Present the multiple moments as a journey, and highlight what you learned within each step along the way. Then, explore how those moments hang together in a series and where especially rich connections exist.

◆ **Twist the kaleidoscope.** Bring it to your documentation work in progress, and use it to identify powerful next moments or practices that might further enrich your learning.

These ideas can help you grow a single moment of documentation into a lengthier journey that offers a deeper understanding of your learning over time. Of course, all of this is dependent on one essential practice: reflection.

*"I've become so much more reflective through this work," Lisa sighs, as amazed by her own learning as I continue to be. Each time I visit with her, we wade further into our curriculum design work, and each experience that we design seems to inspire Lisa's choices as a documentarian, too. Today, we're seated at a table that's covered in artifacts of learning from her current documentation project.*

*"Remember when you told me to teach them the more sophisticated vocabulary words?" she asked, and I nodded. It was a big ask. I knew that Lisa—like most teachers—worried that children this young and inexperienced might struggle to comprehend such big words. Add the learning pause and other disruptions and traumas caused by COVID-19, and these hesitancies are not unexpected. "So I tried. I used the whiteboards, and I had them draw what they thought the words meant, and I was blown away by how well this worked."*

*Lisa documented this and other early learning experiences as children waded into their learning about Greek mythology. At first, she noted progress toward learning targets and goals, but the attention she gave to this work helped her notice things she wouldn't have otherwise, and so, those tiles in her own Documentation Kaleidoscope began to tumble across her line of vision on the daily, and she took good care to steady her vision and remain purposeful in her documentation and reflection work.*

*"I'd wake up in the morning with such great ideas," she marveled. "Documentation made the whole unit exciting to teach, and the kids were into it too," she said. And that was clear as I looked out across the table; she'd turned into a temporary documentation panel. There, students' drawings lived beside their written words, her annotations, and photographs that helped me better understand her practices, their processes, and the products of their learning. You can read this entire case study in my digital documentation notebook.*

## Planning to Reflect Before, During, and After Documentation

It's not the documentation that drives the learning—it's the reflection that happens before, during, and after you document the learning. I find that most documentarians have preferred approaches here, and so, while I share some of my favorites in the appendix, know that your mileage and approach may vary, and that's a beautiful thing—especially if it helps you make meaning well.

I'm a fan of affinity mapping, and I began using it in a bunch of different contexts after reading *Gamestorming: A Playbook for Innovators, Rulebreakers, and Changemakers* (Gray et al., 2010). You'll notice different applications of it in my digital documentation notebook if you're paying close attention. For our purposes as documentarians, affinity mapping invites divergent and then emergent, and finally convergent thinking in service to our learning and work. I typically begin by collecting evidence of learning inside of a moment, a journey, or an expedition. Usually, this evidence isn't organized at first. I drop a bunch of photos into a Google Drive folder. I might add images or videos to my Unrulr profile, or I might build a documentation panel inside a sketchbook, across a wall, or on foam boards that live in my office and garage. I take care not to create connections just yet. I distribute these data randomly and even incoherently inside of whatever analog or digital space I'm keeping for such purposes.

> 🔦 Unrulr is a social learning app where authentic learning moments are captured and interpreted inside of communities where documentation is a culture. I use Unrulr to document my own learning, and I began inviting my Assessment Methods students to do the same in the spring of 2023. I've also used SeeSaw, Storypark, Google Photos, and shared Google Drive folders to invite shared documentation experiences as well. As Aaron Schorn suggests, when learners are able to share their documentation and invite different perspectives, cultures begin to shift. Learning—and studying learning—becomes a valuable, necessary, and routine thing. It's no longer something we do adjacent to what happens outside of school. It becomes a very human endeavor. Multimedia tools that enable learners to capture the whole of their stories are essential to this work.

Next, I begin to cluster these images, videos, and artifacts according to their affinities—or shared characteristics. Finally, I analyze each cluster deeply, defining the concepts at work inside of them. This is where conclusions are drawn. Whenever possible, I invite my students, colleagues, and members of my wider learning network to put their own eyes on these data, notice different affinities, and share their very different perspectives.

If you are a new documentarian, you might use a simple here's what/ so what?/now what? frame to make meaning from all of the documentation gathered. As you gain experience, you might appreciate using more nuanced protocols like those offered by the National School Reform Faculty (2017). As an experienced documentarian, I rely on the free resources shared by Lai-Yee Ho and Alex Limpaecher, the creators of Delve, a collaborative online qualitative data analysis tool that you'll find in the appendix. You'll explore examples of my own work and case studies that illuminate the interpretive processes of different documentarians in my digital documentation notebook. Chapters 7 and 8 will offer much more guidance here as well. Simply, though: Reflection is the way that meaningful interpretation begins. It's important that we become increasingly sophisticated here.

**TLDR (Too Long, Didn't Read)**

1. Documentation is a knotty process, so tools like the Documentation Kaleidoscope matter.
2. Documentation is inductive and deductive, and we shift between these postures as each inquiry unfolds. False starts are common, and they aren't typically failures. Shifting our approach can often help us gain traction when we stall.
3. As we document learning, we take care to make learning visible, capture it, invite diverse perspectives as we interpret our data, and then revise or scrap our plans entirely when they aren't as meaningful as we need them to be.
4. Moments become journeys, and journeys grow into expeditions. The findings from one documentation project typically inspire the start of another, and even when we shift roles and environments, our learning stays with us. It becomes, in many ways, a part of our identities.

**Let's Reflect**

Think about a false start that might have felt like a failure. Were you assuming an inductive or deductive posture? If you had shifted the posture, what would the documentation project have looked like? How would the outcome be different, possibly?

**Try This: Just Right Tools and Invitations**

Use the Documentation Kaleidoscope to begin designing your own project. Keep your greater vision in mind as you plan to document:

**A Moment**

One place and one tightly boundaried moment in time.

**A Journey**

Several moments that unfold in different places over time.

**An Expedition**

A series of journeys that will unfold over the course of multiple months, years, or perhaps—your entire career.

Carry this plan with you into Chapter 5. Here, you will learn more about how to make learning visible in order to document it well.

## References

Gray, D., Brown, S., & Macanufo, J. (2010). *Gamestorming: A playbook for innovators, rulebreakers, and changemakers*. O'Reilly.

Kniep, G. (2008). *Communities that learn, lead, and last: Building and sustaining educational expertise*. Jossey-Bass.

Protocols. National School Reform Faculty. (2017, December 8). https://nsrf-harmony.org/faq-items/protocols/

Stockman, A. (2021). *Creating inclusive writing environments in the K-12 classroom: Reluctance, resistance, and strategies that make a difference*. Routledge, Taylor & Francis Group.

Tolisano, S. R., & Hale, J. A. (2018). *A guide to documenting learning: Making thinking visible, meaningful, shareable, and amplified*. Corwin.

# 5

# How Will You Make Thinking and Learning Visible?

## Preparing to Document Learning

I've learned a great deal about documentation from photographer David Ulrich, the author of *Zen Camera* (2018) and professor and co-director of Pacific New Media Foundation in Honolulu, Hawai'i. These were lessons I'm certain he didn't intend to teach me, as his book was written for photographers whose purposes for taking pictures seem very different from my own—from a distance. Documentation is as much about presence as it is scientific practice, and as a dedicated reader of his writing, I sense that Ulrich feels much the same about photography. This is where I find our Venn Diagram overlapping anyway, and it's the same place I would like you to launch your documentation project from: A place of presence.

As Ulrich teaches us, presence has a vibe—a vitality. It's a heartbeat and a consciousness. It's a sensitivity to our very human perceptions. Presence gentles our hands and steadies our eyes as we enter the spaces where learning is happening. Presence slows our stride and softens our certainty, awakening our creativity. When we are present, we're intentional about what we give our attention, the sustenance we seek and share through our work, the questions we chase, the ones that we offer, and the imprint we leave on the images and recordings we create and the conclusions that are drawn from them. Ulrich calls us to remember that presence humanizes while spectacle debases (Ulrich, 2018, p. 168). If you linger over that for a while, you might

DOI: 10.4324/9781003333241-8

begin to realize how that wisdom can shift our teaching posture entirely and not merely the one we assume as a documentarian of learning.

How often do we make learning a high-impact experience? How often are our assessments of learning invasive, excessive, and immoderate? How often do we hit learners over the head with our theories and practices? This is how Ulrich defines a spectacle. It's what the work of beginning teachers and documentarians often looks like, too.

*When we're intentional about becoming and remaining present in our work, the work becomes more rewarding, both personally and professionally. Lisa Green reminded me of this just yesterday, as I was in the middle of planning this chapter. She sent me the email that you see below, in Figure 5.1. Can you hear her voice there? She's delighted and deeply moved. So much so that she took time out of her day to drop me a message in order to share her joy. This doesn't always happen when we're documenting learning, but Lisa models the best of what it means to be present in our work and to allow ourselves to feel the good stuff.*

*"I wait until the light of the person outshines the light falling on him," Ulrich says about photographing people, and this is how Lisa has come to approach her work. It's how I've come to document my learning about her, too (Ulrich, 2018, p. 53). I share one of Lisa's most thoughtfully designed projects in my digital documentation notebook. It's meaningful. It matters. It's a blatant curation of learning made visible. That case study is light falling on Lisa and I am glad to bring it. This email, though? It captures the light within her, and that light outshines anything that I might orchestrate.*

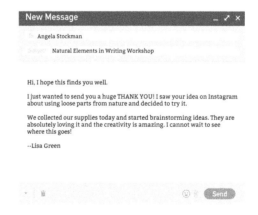

*Figure 5.1—An Email from Lisa Green*

The ideas and tools that follow will help you make learning visible enough to document it. Before you begin lifting them from this page and dropping them into your own world, remember to stay present. Notice when your work is becoming more performative than embodied—more spectacle than sacredness. This happens, and sometimes we have no control over the circumstances that create it. Control what you can, but remain aware of the rest. Notice what's missing, too. After all, "Presence can be understood by its opposite," Ulrich reminds us. "Absence" (2018, p. 163). Another note about this: What follows are insights and ideas that will help you document your own learning about people, places, processes, practices, and the products of learning. As you center yourself inside of your own documentation project, it's important that you remain aware of this positionality and attuned to the fact that your own experiences and perspectives will influence what you notice, how you document your learning, and the interpretations that you create from your findings.

---

In a very real sense, each time you document and share your learning, you will be telling the truth as you see it. Others may have very different interpretations of the same experience—especially those you identify as your subjects. How might you engage them in your process? How might they inform your perspective? More importantly: How might they document their own learning, draw their own conclusions, and share their own stories with those who might benefit most from them? Think on those questions for now, and use your own experiences to imagine what might come next as you engage learners in this process. But know that I wrote this text, especially for you—because I want you to be utterly consumed and enchanted by your own learning. And I want those feelings to become so important to you that you aren't willing to sacrifice them for anything or anyone. Not even your own students. Remember this: You deserve to remain a voracious learner, even as you become a better and better teacher. In fact, there is no becoming a better teacher unless you remain a voracious learner.

---

## The 5 Ps of Documentation

Previous chapters have focused on the *why* and *when* of documentation, but much of this chapter attends to the *how* and the *what*. How might we make learning visible, and what about it is worth documenting? Here, we turn to the outermost ring of the kaleidoscope. Documentarians gather evidence of thinking inside of a moment. When they do this over time, it becomes more and more possible to document deep learning. Thoughtful moments build into journeys that shift the way we think, learn, and work. Some journeys grow into entire expeditions that are career-changing and even life-changing.

We use a variety of tools to curate these observations so that they may rely on them for what they are: Important data that help us construct stories about learning. "But, what do we look for?" I'm often asked. "What are we supposed to document?" I hope that this chapter offers helpful answers to these questions.

In order to document learning, we have to notice it happening. Turning our attention to the people, places, processes, practices, and products inside of our chosen moment sharpens our focus. While it's common for experienced documentarians to speak about the importance of *making* learning visible, but the most humble practitioners I know realize that often, this isn't always something we have to orchestrate. Learning is happening all around us, but we're often too distracted, or perhaps even too biased, to notice it. Table in Figure 5.2 shows where my eyes go and what I try to listen for when I'm documenting learning. My attention typically turns to people, places, processes, practices, and specific products. Consider the questions I've tucked

## Look and Listen

|  People |  Place |  Practice |  Process |  Product |
|---|---|---|---|---|
| Identity | Physical surrounding | Need finding | Cognitive processes | Mastery of learning |
| Interests | Use of light | Research | Creative processes | Mastery of knowledge |
| Funds of knowledge | Use of color | Prototyping | Motivating processes | Growth |
| Wishes and worries | Sound control | Idea generation | Demotivating | Shifts in thinking |
| Aspirations | Scent | Peer review | processes | Shifts in process |
| Performance | Organization | Feedback | Behavioral learning | Shifts in craft |
| Growth | Displays | Revision | processes | Collaborative efforts |
| Interpretations | Documentation | Instruction | Social learning | Reflections |
| Skills | Norms | Self-assessment | processes | Results of design |
| Perseverance | Expectations | Progress monitoring | Collaborative learning | thinking |
| Engagement | Supports | Editing | processes | Results of processes |
| Frustration | Stressors | Craft moves | | and practices |
| Strengths | | | | |

## Wonder

| | |
|---|---|
| What is the relationship between X and Y? | If you change X, how does it influence Y? How does X enhance Y? |
| What does X require of Y? | How does X diminish Y? Is X necessary for Y? |
| What does X afford us that Y does not? | Does X align with Y? |
| What would be gained if we removed X from Y? | When we vary X, how does it affect Y? How do we balance X with Y? |
| How is X tempered by Y? | What is the effect of X and Y on Z? |

*Figure 5.2—Riffing Off of Trevor Aleo's Work*

into that illustration as well. They might serve you well as you begin taking and then—with experience—*making* photos, videos, and other artifacts of learning with purposeful and even artful intention.

This is an important bit of nuance: Our perspectives and involvement with our subjects shift from one moment to another. It can also deepen over time. When we're just beginning, when time is tight, or when we're not quite sure what we might be looking for in a learning moment, we tend to simply take photos, recordings, and artifacts that serve as evidence of learning. We try to capture everything we can, without much discretion. Then, we return to our collection of photos later to search for meaning. Experienced documentarians are typically a bit more intentional and nimble. They often enter a learning experience with a distinct set of purposes; they've anticipated how their documentation work might unfold, and they're ready to shift postures and practices as needed. Experienced documentarians know when to slow down and linger over their learning. They're a bit more selective about what they document and how. They reflect and make learning stories in the moment as it unfolds, and what they learn changes how they teach—as they are teaching. I find myself pivoting between these two distinct postures often on any given day: Sometimes, I document widely and wait to review and reflect. Sometimes, I document purposefully, reflecting on my feet, in process, and in ways that immediately change my practice. Both approaches are useful, as long as reflection ensures that all documentation efforts have been worthwhile. More on that in Chapter 7.

## Documenting What We Learn About and From People

Documenting what I learn *about* learners and—more importantly—*from* them has been some of the most rewarding work of my career. Certainly, I document my learning about other people too, but it's the learners I serve who compel me most, and I'll assume that if you're reading this book, the same might be true for you.

This is the kind of documentation that has had the most profound influence on my thinking and my behavior. It also deepens my self-awareness, humbles me, and helps me realize that I don't have to have all of the answers or be a savior to anyone. These are some of the purposes I carry into this specific sort of documentation work and the practices that I value most, too:

◆ I document what learners reveal about their identities, their interests, the funds of knowledge they bring into our community, and their social and emotional strengths and needs.

- ◆ I notice and note their wishes and their worries, their aspirations, goals, and plans.
- ◆ I document their performance as they pursue standards, outcomes, and objectives set for them and those they've set for themselves.
- ◆ I document their interpretations of events that we've both experienced, including learning, as we've documented it separately and together.
- ◆ I document what I notice about what John Hattie refers to as a learner's skill (what they come to us already able to do or achieve), their will (or their attitudes, frames of mind, or tendencies as learners), and the thrill they gain from the learning experience (what motivates them). As Hattie asserts, these three learning inputs, which are also learning outputs, serve as skills that can be leveraged at different points in the learning experience for effect. For instance, effective learners draw upon their prior skills as they acquire new knowledge at a surface level, but as they begin to deepen and consolidate this knowledge, their will has a greater effect on their success, and it's the thrill of learning that makes for the successful transfer of knowledge to new and uncommon contexts (Hattie, 2023, pp. 340–355).

It's important to note that when I think about documenting what I learn from and about people, I consider what I'm learning about myself, too. Exploring the preceding bullet points through that lens changes my purpose and my perspective a great deal. Documenting what I learn about myself beside the evidence I'm gathering from and about other people is often quite revealing, too. Notebooks and sketchbooks are useful for these purposes. You'll find examples in my digital documentation notebook.

*"What does it mean to be the documentor?" Kenisha asks when I explain that this book will be written for teachers who are interested in documenting their own learning, but that more books are needed that guide children to document themselves, too.*

*It's important, as you put your plans into action, that you understand and are honest with yourself about your purposes and your point of view.*

*"What does it mean to tell someone else's story?" Kenisha continues, and we both agree: This is dangerous*

*and even harmful work. But when teachers and students each document their own learning—separate from but beside one another—powerful discoveries are made.*

*"We need to maintain an inquisitive stance whenever we document our learning about students," she reminds me. "Students are often compliant. They'll agree with us just because we're the adults—the teachers. They may even come from cultures that have taught them it's disrespectful to do otherwise." So when we share our interpretations of their learning rather than simply asking questions, looking, or listening, learners may simply validate our conclusions even if they don't necessarily agree with them.*

*"So much depends on the moments we capture too," she concludes. "What if we only captured a moment of struggle inside of a learning experience that included many successes?"*

*Unless we talk with learners and invite them to document their own learning, we miss so much.*

*Consider how you might attend to these realities in your own classroom or context, and remember: This book was written for teachers—for you alone. What would it mean to engage and support learners in their own documentation work? What tools and resources currently exist for this? You'll find my favorites in the appendix.*

## Documenting What We Learn From and About Places

Loris Malaguzzi, founder and leader of the world-renowned municipal preschools of Reggio Emilia, Italy, aligned his thinking with Soviet psychologist Lev Vygotsky's social development theory, which asserts that child development and learning ability are socially and culturally dependent. This contributed to Malaguzzi's assertion that the learning environment functioned as a third teacher, and it was this assertion that inspired me to make several trips to Reggio Emilia, where my study tours were dedicated to the exploration of that particular understanding (Strong-Wilson & Ellis, 2007). These visits taught me much that I've been able to bring home, adapt inside of my very western work, and use to improve learning outcomes for my own students and the teachers I continue to serve as a consultant. The images you find in my digital documentation notebook exemplify some of the ways that I document my learning about environment or place. This is how that often happens:

- ◆ I note the features of the physical environment. They include the physical surroundings in which learning takes place, such as the classroom itself, libraries, gymnasiums, auditoriums, music and art rooms, and outdoor spaces. We take note of the arrangement of furniture, the use of light, color, and the organization of materials. I take note of documentation and displays, how learning and evidence of it is shared, and the types of engagement that the physical environment is designed to support.

◆ I also document what we see, hear, and experience within digital learning environments, too. I study how virtual learning spaces are organized, ease of navigation, and accessibility. I capture evidence of how the environment shapes the way that learners engage with content, instructors, and one another, too.

◆ I notice and take note of the cultural environment, gathering evidence of the norms, values, beliefs, and expectations that shape teaching and learning experiences.

◆ I look and listen for evidence of psychological or emotional supports and stressors within the environment. I document what we see and hear within the learning environment that might serve learners' mental health and well-being and the growth of their dispositions and mindsets.

## Documenting What We Learn From and About Processes

This involves noticing how people accomplish things. Rather than focusing on the attributes of person, place, product, or practice, we make a dedicated study of processes instead. You'll find examples of these approaches in my digital documentation notebook.

◆ I often document learners' cognitive processes. These are the mental processes used to perceive, attend to, absorb, and integrate new information. For instance, problem-solving is a cognitive process.

◆ I gather evidence of creative processes as they unfold as well. As learners engage in inquiry work, design and make things, or engage in the written writing process, documentation helps me notice and take note of the unique ways they approach their work, what works, and what does not.

◆ I might also pay attention to what motivates and demotivates learners. As I explained previously, my first book, *Make Writing* (Stockman, 2015) was my effort to invite diverse perspectives around what I was noticing about writers who initially presented as resistant in my workshops and studios and how unexpected practices, processes, and the environment we created together seemed to be motivating them.

If I'd been holding the Documentation Kaleidoscope in my hand on the day that Max began building their story, I would have adjusted it to focus squarely on understanding a person by documenting their process. Specifically, I hoped to better understand what motivated Max by documenting the very unique storymaking process they were using when given abundant choice and control over the materials.

Instead of taking a seat beside their classmates who were composing characters and settings with written words inside of composition books or across screens, Max was standing at the back of the room building a setting with LEGO, creating characters that would quickly engage with it, and bantering to himself through it all. Once their characters were created, they made them interact with one another, and suddenly, the whole scene started coming to life.

Max was immersed in the story, role-playing as they lifted one character into action and then assuming the voice of another as it responded. Pieces of their setting began to move and morph, and it was quite clear that this young designer had been making this story for quite some time before they ever entered the room. This moment happened long before I ever visited Reggio Emilia, but as I write about it now, I'm reminded all over again about what the pedagogistas reminded us of so often there. Every material has its own language, and when we use them, they teach us how to speak it.

"Children know the language of clay," one of them suggested to me once.

And too soon, they forget.

I'm brought back to this moment every time I bring loose parts into a middle school classroom for the very first time. Learners this age often mess around with the materials for a long time before they do anything that seems intentional. They make simple things, feign frustration, and even start throwing materials across tables at one another.

"I can't use those materials in my class because the kids get off task," too many teachers tell me.

"But they don't remember how to do anything useful with it at first," Reggio teachers might say. "They're playing with it and one another, in order to figure out how it works—in order to relearn this language that was taken from them not so long ago."

This is what I often tell teachers when they begin to lose patience with students who appear disruptive in my writing studio or in classrooms where we're only beginning to make writing. When we practice patience and try to document those unexpected moments carefully—storyboarding the experience with our cameras and capturing sticky note annotations— we can often notice the exact moment when their skills return to them. We can often document their return to the language of loose parts and play and multimodal expression. The energy in the room shifts, and so does their focus. And it is glorious.

While I didn't have the opportunity to document Max's first moments making writing quite as carefully as I would if I were in his company now, I did take abundant notes. I did confer with them extensively that summer and for a few more to come. And I do know this: If I hadn't been willing to be a student instead of a teacher in those moments, I may not have realized the skills that Max was bringing into my studio. I would have assumed they were not interested in writing. I would have assumed that they were struggling. I would have seen deficits. Documentation enabled me to notice such incredible strengths.

The fact is that Max had been building his story for ages before he ever brought those LEGO into my studio. They had plenty of background knowledge and lots of practice building complex worlds and characters with loose parts. As the summer went on and we challenged them to transition from telling their story with LEGO to using labels and then—soon enough—written words, their certainty about the quality of their story had already been established. They knew it was good because he had the chance to write and share it with materials before we ever pushed them to produce print. So, when we eventually did, their will was strong. Their mindset was positive, and the use of labels, sentence frames, and sticky notes made the process accessible for them. They were excited. Hopeful. Able to endure a bit of productive frustration on their way from making to producing written words. And then later the following summer, when WORD 2010 was released and some of the teachers in our studio were confused by all of the changes, Max offered to run a training session for all of us. I think they were six years old at the time.

I still felt the weight of the Documentation Kaleidoscope in my hand as each of these initial learning moments led into one another. I wasn't certain how to use it with any level of precision then, but working with Max and other young writers in my studio over those first years rooted me in new and exciting purposes. I wanted to remember those writers and the surprising things they were doing. I wanted to understand those processes better. I wanted to use them to serve other young writers well.

◆   I document metacognitive processes as well. This refers to a learner's awareness and understanding of their own process or—as some describe it—their thinking about their thinking. This is often inspired by reflection, which I try to make time for before, during, and after learning each time I teach. You'll find some of my favorite prompts in the appendix.

◆ I also document evidence of concept acquisition, when and how learners relate concepts to one another and deepen their understanding of them, and how they transfer the concepts attained in one context to another one that's entirely new. If you have read my previous book, *The Writing Workshop Teacher's Guide to Multimodal Composition*, then you know that Julie Stern, Kayla Duncan, Trevor Aleo, and Krista Ferraro have had a significant influence on my own learning about teaching for transfer (Stern et al., 2021). You'll find examples of how I've applied it in my digital documentation notebook.

## Documenting What We Learn From and About Practices

Practices are often based on established principles, standards, or guidelines that have been proven to be effective. Usually developed over time and through experience, practices offer promising frameworks for approaching specific kinds of learning experiences. For instance, while some might argue that the writing process is a linear set of steps that we move through as we brainstorm, draft, seek feedback, revise, and then edit our work, I would offer that that is just one of many different ways to *practice* the process of writing. Documenting my learning taught me this. Here are a few other ways in which I document my learning about practices:

◆ I pay attention to how writers practice idea generation and then the way they develop their ideas, capturing evidence along the way. I often notice that documenting my learning about practices often finds me shifting from deductive to inductive postures as learners pique my interest by doing things that are quite unexpected. I share a story about this with examples in my digital documentation notebook.

◆ I document the way that learners prototype or draft their ideas. When I make our learning targets clear, I find that this offers students greater freedom to express their ideas multimodally. This makes prewriting and drafting incredibly productive and rewarding.

◆ I also notice and take note of how they practice peer review and the giving and receiving of feedback. I invite self-assessment and a great deal of metacognitive reflection here as well. It was documentation that taught me how to improve the way I coached peer review and improved my peer-editing invitations. I share a powerful example and my current approach in my digital documentation notebook.

◆ I document evidence of revision, editing, and how learners distinguish them from one another.

- ◆ I notice and make note of the way that writers practice specific craft moves, for effect.
- ◆ I also document the practices that designers use when they assume these different postures: need finding, problem defining, research, prototyping, testing, and launching. Again, establishing clear goals or outcomes gives learners permission to use—and share—diverse practices and expertise. Documentation helps us notice the best of these contributions so that we can leverage them ourselves.

As a young teacher, my attitude about the constraints that standards impose made for quite a bit of unproductive struggle. When I began documenting my learning about the influence of loose parts inside of compositional processes, it taught me something quite surprising, though: Constraint matters, and when I hold my standard or learning target close—when I keep it conscious—it's actually quite freeing.

For instance, if writers have investigated a variety of stories and they've defined narrative structure as somebody wanted, but so (Macon et al., 1994), then they might use any materials or modes of expression to represent the ideas that live within each bit of the form. This makes the process far more accessible for many writers, and it also protects the complexity of their ideas. When I push writers to keyboards, pencils, and pens too quickly, they lower the complexity of their ideas to match their print power. When I invite them to represent the structure of any form using familiar materials and modes of expression, they share their most sophisticated works. And then we take care to protect their architecture as they transition from making to writing.

I can't help but wonder how Hattie's (2023) VL model of the breadth and depth of learning might be relevant here (p. 341). Hattie suggests that learners who bring previously acquired skills to new and surface level learning are better able to "know that." In other words, their previous skills help them acquire and consolidate new, related knowledge and skills. However, it's their will that draws them into deeper levels of learning where they "learn how" by connecting concepts and skills, and consolidating and practicing what they've learned. Ultimately, deep learners are able to transfer this knowledge to new and uncommon contexts. This "knowing-with" as Hattie refers to it—an often thrilling experience—is the hallmark of deep learning (pp. 345–355).

My interpretation of each moment I revisit inside of this greater learning expedition is so different now, having read and learned more about it in the years after I shared my first set of findings in *Make Writing: 5 Teaching Strategies that Turn Writer's Workshop into a Makerspace*

(Stockman, 2015). I'm realizing how skillful writers are when I invite them to use familiar materials and modes to represent the surface of their ideas. This builds their confidence while deepening their conceptual knowledge about the structure of a form (such as story) and its essential elements. They have the will, in these contexts, to stick with their storymaking even as I invite them to begin producing print—something that certainly frustrates many of them. And then, invitations to exhibit their works in process, share their expertise with other teachers, and be treated like the experts and instructors they truly are within and even beyond our community engage them even further. They share new and even innovative ideas freely, knowing that we're interested in watching them give them a go. They aren't interested in completing assignments in order to check boxes on some to-do list. They're thrilled to be learning with us. Teaching us. Discovering what they're good at and ready to try next. I'm not certain what Hattie would think about any of this. In fact, my understanding of his model might be entirely wrong. I'm still learning myself, and I'll keep documenting my way to better understanding. Have a peek at some of this work in my documentation notebook.

## Documenting What We Learn From and About Products

When I think about products, my attention turns to documents, artifacts, interviews, and observations. Documents are records of communication that I create during a learning experience. Here, I'm thinking about the annotated records and conference notes I produce as I'm working with learners. Artifacts are objects that can be found within the learning environment itself. Pages from a writer's notebook or ticket-out-the-door reflections are good examples here. So are anchor charts and mentor texts. Whenever I ask a learner a question—in any context—it can serve as an interview. And when I take note of what I see within a product, I'm relying on observation. Here are some of the ways I document what I learn from and about products, such as these:

◆ I gather evidence of mastery of knowledge or skills. This often enables me to scoop data from learning experiences and creative environments rather than bringing learning to a halt in order to test. You'll find my favorite strategies, beside examples from classrooms I've taught in, in my digital documentation notebook.

◆ I also document growth by capturing products of learning at different points in time or as learners evolve from apprenticeship to mastery. Although it's not always possible, I find that having a laser-like focus is helpful here. It's not always productive to document the whole of a product as it evolves over time, but if I know which piece of it compels me most, I can tighten my aperture in ways that make my learning more purposeful and productive.

◆ Capture shifts in design thinking, process, and craft by studying how products evolve as well. I've left a collection of images that illustrate this phenomenon in my digital notebook.

◆ Documenting how learners communicate individually and collaborate together is powerful, too. It was my friend Erin Quinn who introduced me to sociograms. These graphical representations of relationships display the connections and interactions between members of a group, providing insights into the social structure, dynamics, and patterns of relationships among the group's members. Sociograms typically use various symbols, lines, and nodes to represent individuals and the nature of their relationships. Nodes or circles represent individuals, and lines or arrows indicate the relationships between them. The nature of the lines or arrows can vary depending on the type of relationship being depicted. For example, a solid line may represent a friendship or positive relationship, while a dashed line may represent a conflict or negative relationship. I often use them to examine communication patterns between learners who are engaged in collaborative work. This reveals interesting features in group social dynamics as well as key individuals, the strength or weakness of certain relationships, and patterns of influence.

◆ Reflective work is worth curating at any moment and over time, too. I typically invite learners to reflect before a learning experience begins, during the process, and after the experience has ended. You'll find examples of this in my digital documentation notebook. My understanding of reflection and my ability to facilitate it has evolved quite a bit over the years because I am a documentarian. I say more about this in Chapter 7, where you will also find prompts and protocols that you may use or adapt for your own purposes.

## Making Thinking Visible in a Single Moment

Thinking can happen independent of learning, but learning is always dependent on thinking. Consider this: When I am thinking about ideas for this chapter, I'm sifting through my prior knowledge, making decisions, reasoning, and contemplating possibilities. I may begin to define what I'd like to learn, but that learning does not yet have to happen in order for me to be thinking within the moment. Learning refers to the acquisition of new knowledge, skills, insights, attitudes, or behaviors. This usually happens as we engage in inquiry work, gain new experiences, or teach. It involves a change in our existing knowledge or a shift in behavior that typically unfolds over time—scene-by-scene—in different settings. This is where thinking is made visible one small moment at a time. When we take care to document thinking scene-by-scene, studying learning over time becomes more meaningful and efficient. There are many ways to accomplish this. In this chapter, I hope to introduce you to a few favorites that scale, so that you may experiment with them in your own context.

---

If you are not yet familiar with Harvard's Project Zero, you'll want to put this book aside for a bit and follow the link you find in the appendix to their Thinking Routine Toolbox. There, you'll find a robust collection of protocols intended to scaffold learners' thinking while making it visible. You may search by subject, thinking disposition or competence, or specific project (related to their work). These routines are easy to lift and drop into any number of different learning situations, and learners can use them repeatedly without tiring of them because they feel and work differently as the content of each learning experience changes.

I use these routines as a teacher, and I rely on them as a learner, too. They make my documentation processes far more rewarding. If you think about any learning experience as a story, then learners serve as characters and the classroom, studio, or workshop becomes a setting. The practices, processes, and skills we experiment with as we learn and make things together drive the plot of our story, but the thinking often remains invisible unless we take care to illuminate it. Doing this adds depth to our learning stories. Rather than merely capturing evidence of people, places, practices, processes, and products inside of any scene, capturing our thinking about them helps us move out of the shallows and into much deeper storymaking and telling. Thinking routines enable this well.

---

Project Zero's See, Think, and Wonder routine offers a simple but powerful way to begin. It's grounded in three questions that I carry into nearly every learning scene I enter: *What do I see?*, *What do I think about that?*, and *What does it make me wonder?* These questions are easy to hold onto, they activate the documentarian me, and they also engage me in the moment in ways I might not be, otherwise. This makes the whole of my work more rewarding. It also helps me connect one learning scene to another, over time. Thinking routines have made me a far more conscious practitioner, and they've kept me curious and humble, too. When I'm tired, frustrated, or bordering on burnout, thinking routines help me teach and learn beyond the surface of any single story. They push me to see past the plot, challenging me to tease out themes, messages, lessons, and my students' actual perceptions rather than the assumptions I may be making about them. You know: The real learning.

## Making Learning Visible Over Time

Making thinking visible in a moment and documenting what we see and hear prepares us to begin studying learning over time. Aaron Schorn describes collections of moments as journeys, and I think this is a perfect way to define them as well. A journey might unfold over an hour or within the space of an afternoon. It might unfold over an entire day, or a week, or perhaps—even a month. Journeys are often planned experiences, but this isn't always the case. Some of my favorite journeys were invitations that I stumbled upon quite accidentally simply because I am a documentarian.

Whenever I document a journey, coding helps me make meaning from the images, artifacts, and recordings I gather over time. You'll find a variety of common approaches in Figure 5.3. My process is a relatively simple one that I've adapted from the work of many practitioners over the years, including Lisa Given (2008), and most recently LaiYee Ho (2021) and Alex Limpaecher (2018). We will take a much deeper dive into qualitative data analysis and coding in Chapter 7 as well. I will be honest though: I'm still very much a beginner here.

- ◆ I begin by creating a simple display of images, documents, artifacts, and transcripts from audio or video recordings. Then, I immerse myself in these data, refamiliarizing myself with moments that have passed and often, noticing things I didn't when I was documenting each of them. I always invite others to have a peek as well, and I do my best to glean perspectives from different kinds of people— including and especially those I'm trying to serve better.
- ◆ This initial review helps me identify key ideas, critical concepts, potential patterns, themes, and questions worth pursuing further. I create simple codes for each of them, and then, I begin using them to label associated elements in my data. These codes help me begin interpreting these data, and as they become more robust, they also serve as a reference guide that helps to ensure consistency and reliability in my analysis. Some of my codes are descriptive, while

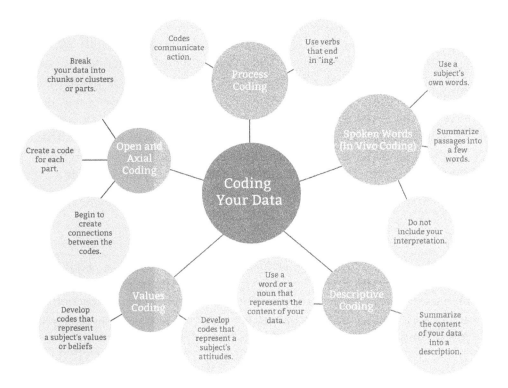

*Figure 5.3—Coding Your Data*

others are conceptual or theoretical. You can see examples of this and learn more about how these different codes compare in my digital documentation notebook.

◆ When I'm analyzing a single moment, my codes remain relatively fixed. It's when I begin connecting moments and their related data that my coding becomes a bit more iterative. I modify or add codes as needed each time I bring a new bit of documentation into a collection. This helps me notice and study new patterns and themes. Diverse perspectives are important here as well, and again, I invite others into the work.

◆ Once I've exhausted the coding process, I interpret the data further, in order to develop even more meaningful insights. I explore the relationships between codes, comparing different bits of documentation and even segments of whole photos, artifacts, or recordings. Theories begin to emerge at this point, and I share them as widely as I can, owning the fact that these ideas are often highly experimental and encouraging others to test and even, push back against them. This is why I publish my books. It's also why I work hard to build deep and lasting professional relationships with others on social media. My network is full of sharp minds, those who share my enthusiasm for teaching and learning, and critical friends who help me check my biases. I'll explore the purpose of diverse perspective-taking and practices that support it well in Chapter 7. For now, know that coding helps us reap tremendous rewards from our journeys and expeditions. Tinker with the process I've described here in your own way before digging into greater challenges. You'll find additional resources and tools that can support your work as a beginner or a more experienced documentarian in the appendix.

---

**?** How might data-driven teachers and leaders find value in pedagogical documentation? Coding these qualitative data helps those responsible for improving performance see the potential impact of instruction on learning outcomes. This is something we've far too often relied upon testing to accomplish. When I'm hired to improve performance in schools, we begin by analyzing multiple points of quantitative data because, often, those are the only data we have. Improving those results requires us to teach and assess in healthier and far more engaging ways, though. Pedagogical documentation is not the icing on any cake we serve in data team meetings. It is the cake.

---

*Angelique explains that her own documentation work developed new and unexpected dimensions when she began capturing her own learning as a literacy coach. Her story speaks to the intersections that can develop between students, parents, teachers, and learning leaders in any system.*

*Rather than merely inviting children to document their own learning and then, documenting ours as instructors beside them, we might extend invitations to families, and also: Document our learning as adult learning facilitators as well.*

*"Imagine what can happen if I'm not only documenting my learning about students but if I do the same as an instructional coach who is constantly learning from teachers, too?" she asks, and I find myself nodding and considering something else:*

*So often, coaching relationships are undermined by power imbalances within the coach-teacher relationship and the system as a whole. I know this from experience, as someone who has tried—sometimes unsuccessfully—to prevent this from happening. When I reflect on my own experiences in the wake of my conversation with Angelique, I realize something interesting: When I've taken care to document my learning as a coach and make that work visible to those I'm partnered with, they do tend to see me as a learner rather than an expert. I am received as a partner positioned beside them in the work. This hasn't been the case when I coach without documenting my learning. Writing this book for all of you is dropping new stones into my own shoes, and this is an example of that. I'm grateful for it, too.*

## TLDR (Too Long, Didn't Read)

1. Planning what we will document often turns our attention to people, places, processes, practices, and products. Defining which of those we will take care to pay specific attention to and capture evidence of can make our documentation efforts more productive.
2. When we observe and document our learning about people, we often pay close attention to expressions of their identities, their funds of knowledge, strengths, and interests. We glean their perspectives about their own learning and ours as well. We invite their interpretations of our documentation, and we document that, too. When we learn about people, we document their progress toward goals, learning outcomes, standards, and yes, performance. We also capture what we notice about the skills they bring into the learning environment, their will, and the thrill they experience as learners (Hattie, 2023, pp. 340–355).
3. When we document places, we capture features of physical and digital environments, as well as evidence of the norms, values, and beliefs of those who learn there. We document what we notice about culturally sustaining design and the physical and emotional supports available to community members who gather in each space.
4. Documenting processes turn our attention to cognitive, metacognitive, and creative processes that engage learners in surface, deep, or transfer-level work (Stern et al., 2021).
5. Products reveal much about mastery, and when we compare them side-by-side over the course of a learning experience, they can also demonstrate growth or the achievement of transfer. Such comparisons can also reveal shifts in thinking, process, or practice.

6. Idea generation and development, prototyping, drafting, peer-review, feedback exchanges, editing, revision, craft moves, collaboration, reflection, and design thinking all rely on practices, and documenting them at work helps us learn more about all of them.
7. Coding enables us to notice, define, and build theories about the patterns we notice in the data we capture.

### Let's Reflect

Consider the documentation opportunities you see in Figure 5.2. Then, reflect: Have you documented for any of these purposes before? How would you describe those experiences? Are any of these invitations calling to you right now? Why is that? If you were to begin a new project or continue one in progress, how could this tool best support those efforts?

### Try This: Just Right Tools and Invitations

Use the tool provided in Figure 5.2 to plan or refine your documentation project. Determine whether you will capture a single moment or document a lengthier journey or complete expedition. Then, consider whether you will capture observations about people, places, processes, practices, or products. What will you look and listen for? What questions might you pursue? The decisions you make here will make what your next experiences with this book more productive.

## References

Given, L. M. (2008). *The Sage Encyclopedia of qualitative research methods*. Sage.

Hattie, J. (2023). *Visible learning: The sequel*. Taylor & Francis Ltd.

Ho, L. (2021). *How to use grounded theory to discover new ideas*. Quality Research Consultants Association.

Limpaecher, A. (2018, December 12). Who needs qualitative research when you have numbers. *Medium*. https://medium.com/delve/from-research-hater-to-advocate-e8e43e4ec889

Macon, J. M., Bewell, D., & Vogt, M. E. (1994). *Responses to literature*. International Reading Association.

Stern, J. H., Ferraro, K. F., Duncan, K., Aleo, T., Hattie, J., & Zhao, Y. (2021). *Learning that transfers: Designing curriculum for a changing world*. Corwin.

Stockman, A. (2015). *Make writing: 5 teaching strategies that turn writer's workshop into a maker space*. Times 10 Publications.

Strong-Wilson, T., & Ellis, J. (2007). Children and place: Reggio Emilia's environment as third teacher. *Theory into Practice, 46*(1), 40–47.

Ulrich, D. (2018). *Zen camera: Creative awakening with daily practice in photography*. Watson-Guptill.

# 6

# How Will You Document Thinking and Learning?

If you're a new documentarian, then you should know that your first experiences will likely feel uncertain. You may not know what your greater vision is just yet. You may be unclear about your purposes, what you hope to learn, what's worth documenting, or which tools might be best. And no matter how thoughtful you are in your planning, your initial efforts to make thinking visible and then capture it may not offer you the return on your investment that you thought they would.

This is all quite common.

There are approaches I wish I'd used when I was new to this work, and they're still a necessary part of my repertoire now. I've just become more intuitive about using them, and they work adjacent to other practices that I've

Here's one bit of perspective that serves us well in any context:
Anytime you feel yourself floundering a bit, ground yourself in the moment, quiet your mind, and simply notice what you see. That's it. That's the simplest way to begin, gain traction, or steady your process when it feels like your documentation project is blowing up entirely or perhaps becoming an unproductive waste of time. Just notice what you see, and as Davide Ulrich suggests, try not to worry too much about making "good" photos, recordings, or annotations. Instead, just see what you see (Ulrich, 2018, p. 13).

DOI: 10.4324/9781003333241-9

adopted over time, as documentation has become less of a thing that I do and more a way of being. This chapter will support your beginning and your growth over time. Return to it often as your purposes and experiences evolve. Let it serve as your companion and mentor each time you plan a new project or encounter knots in one that's currently in motion.

We shouldn't be afraid to get off track as documentarians, either. When plans unravel, we're often better able to see inside of them. When our projects get off course, we're forced to travel unbeaten paths, and the sights we see along the way inspire new, different, and sometimes brilliant insights. When things don't go as we intended them to, it's easy to assume we've failed. If we're truly documenting our learning though, shifts in plans, purposes, and thinking are essential. If we're doing it well, false starts are formative experiences. Rather than deeming any project or path you're traveling along a failure, recognize stalls and upsets for what they are: the lessons and learning we showed up for in the first place. We begin to welcome the detours and anticipate sliding into deep ditches along the way. We begin to realize that often, this is where our best discoveries are made.

If you're a writer, then you understand this phenomenon well. Quick wins are nice, and I love being able to fast-draft a solid piece. I rarely learn anything from those experiences, though. I'm simply sharing what I already know a bit about. It's the tougher projects—the ones I'm less certain about—that give me a good workout. I may not appreciate the discomfort while I'm enduring it, but when it's over? I'm better for it. I've learned something along the way.

Experienced documentarians know that as long as they remain disciplined, the process of documentation will undo any knots they encounter in the process. When documentation becomes a habit rather than something we simply do once in a while, it rewards us for our efforts. It becomes a constant companion, a candid critical friend, and an engaging travel partner who points out the scenery in our peripheral vision, mitigating any threat of highway hypnosis. If we're willing to shift our gaze a bit, our practice is often better for it.

Over time, disciplined documentarians become increasingly absorbed by the process and engaged by the full kaleidoscope of learning opportunities available to them. Their work becomes less about traveling the straight path they've carved into any map and more about what they choose to pay attention to and how they choose to see and remember it. This is rewarding work, even when it doesn't return the results we anticipate. This is how documentation keeps us hungry. It's how we remain dedicated practitioners. This is how we begin to define and often—redefine—our teaching identities, our greater vision for the difference we will make, and our expectations about what teaching will give to us as well. Each community we serve, administrator we're led by, and classroom we teach within is one chapter in a far greater journey. The lessons they teach us contribute to the overarching themes that will emerge at the end of our greatest expeditions. They are not the whole of our story, though. This is what centers me when I'm feeling disillusioned or disenfranchised. I want the same for you. So, how do we begin once we have some idea of our vision and purposes? How do we document thinking and learning?

## Choosing an Inductive or Deductive Approach

Previous chapters of this book invited you to begin defining a greater vision and clear purposes for a documentation project. I also invited you to use the Documentation Kaleidoscope to begin refining your thinking and making meaningful plans. If you're a new documentarian, I would recommend a simple start. Begin with a deductive process, and focus your study inside of a single moment. If you're eager to document a journey or an expedition, using a deductive process may make that more manageable for you, too. If you're an experienced documentarian, I've left some of my favorite approaches and invitations in the appendix for you. I hope they refresh your practice and reignite your enthusiasm for this work. I've left examples from my own beginnings in my digital documentation notebook, too. Some are gleaned from my initial efforts to document my learning twenty or more years ago. Other stories are quite current. I'd love to know what you notice when you study them side-by-side. Come find me on social if you're willing to share.

Will you document to remember someone or something, to better understand either, or to be of better service as a result? Do you anticipate limiting your study to a single moment that attends to one of those purposes, or are you willing and ready to shift postures as a greater journey or an entire expedition unfolds? And where will you focus your documentation efforts initially? Will you steady your gaze upon certain people (perhaps yourself or your students), places, practices, processes, or the products of learning? These are the questions you will want to sit with a bit before you move forward.

## Capturing What Matters

Returning to the outer ring of the kaleidoscope is helpful here. If you remember, documenting people, places, practices, processes, and products of learning often leads to meaningful discoveries. Once you enter any learning environment, those tiles will tumble in and out of so many different positions, though. It can feel a bit disorienting. It's hard to know—in any moment—what would be best to capture. Planning ahead is helpful, but if we take a closer look at each of these tiles, we can begin to anticipate how they might tilt inside of our best-laid plans, changing our view of the learning landscape entirely. Understanding the affordances of each element prepares us for the unexpected, enabling us to focus and then—refocus—our vision and our documentation efforts accordingly.

In the spring of 2023, I introduced the students in my Assessment Methods in Education class to learning walls. Conceptualized by teacher, coach, and literacy leader Jessica Vance (2023), they enable communities of learners to co-construct meaning in incredibly visual and spatial ways. The group begins by posting big ideas and intentions for learning on the wall before engaging in sustained inquiry work that produces artifacts worth adding. Sketchnotes, illustrations, articles, and sticky note reflections live adjacent to one another on the wall, and as learners review and consider them, connections are made. The wall becomes a dynamic mind-map of sorts—shifting shape and enabling deeper collaborative connections. As you might imagine, I went into this lesson with clear intentions and a solid documentation plan. By the end of my lesson, learners would be able to describe how learning walls might serve as powerful assessment tools. I intended to document moments in order to better understand my students' experience with the learning wall we were creating together and its relevance to some of the big ideas we were studying in class, including visible learning and formative assessment. I planned to pose some pointed questions, challenging learners to offer written responses on sticky notes that would be added to the board. I also prepared them to draw their thinking by introducing Dave Gray's visual alphabet—you'll find it linked in the appendix. I had a plan: I would document a moment in order to understand people (my students) and, more specifically, what they'd learned.

Only something completely unexpected happened.

The night before I taught this lesson, I happened upon a massive box of scented markers at our local Target. They were the exact brand I loved as a kid, and so, of course, I bought them. And I brought them to class. And my twenty-something-year-old students had an absolute blast building, connecting, and then remixing their ideas together while choosing the perfect scent for each amendment to our learning wall. I've never smiled so hard inside of a lesson before, and as the volume of their laughter rose high above any intention I'd set for the day, I couldn't help but begin to capture it. I documented what I initially came for as well, but that kaleidoscope tilted quickly in my hands that morning, and because I took the detour, I learned so much more along the way. And my documentation efforts were better for it. Have a

### Learning Opportunities, Approaches, and Tools and Platforms to Consider

| Focus | Learning Opportunity | Tools and Platforms to Consider | Examples |
|---|---|---|---|
| People | Interviewing people is one of the best ways to learn more about their identities, values, beliefs, and attitudes. It also teaches us much about how they think, their needs and interests, and their interpretations of experiences. | Speech-to-text apps enable us to record the interview in a non-invasive way while producing transcripts that we can easily skim, scan, and interpret. | Microsoft Dictate, Google Docs Voice Typing, Apple Dictation, Windows Speech, Otter.ai, Dragon, and Amazon Transcribe |
| Places | Photography enables us to capture evidence of the norms, expectations, supports, and stressors in an environment. | Digital photography is efficient and allows us to capture and save images in albums that align to distinct codes. | Google Photos, Apple iCloud, Amazon Prime Photos, Photobucket, Dropbox FlickR.

Electing to use captioning when we video record enables us to code and interpret these data well.

Unrulr, SeeSaw, and Storypark are documentation apps that enable multimedia documentation. |
| Processes or Practices | Video helps us capture cognitive, creative, social, emotional, behavioral, collaborative, motivating, or demotivating processes. It can also allow us to capture design, instructional, and compositional practices. | Video invites learners to capture processes or practices bit-by-bit or across one uninterrupted stretch of time. Storyboards with photos are useful as well but are a bit more disruptive to the learning process because they require learners to stop and snap multiple images. We can set devices to record and left them relatively unattended. | |
| Products | Documenting the products of learning can help us assess and understand mastery. Comparing process works to their related final products can help us understand and assess growth over time. We can also study shifts in thinking and process this way. | Whenever possible, it is helpful to collect the actual artifacts of learning--including its products. Photography is helpful here when the products of learning are static. Video helps us capture more dynamic products. | |

*Figure 6.1—Learning Opportunities, Approaches, and Tools and Platform to Consider*

peek inside my documentation notebook if you'd like to see how this learning moment connected to a far greater journey.

When you're an experienced documentarian, you're accustomed to curves in the road. When you're just trying to get your legs beneath you and learning actually disrupts your documentation plans, it's easy to assume things are unraveling, though. They aren't. You simply need to shift your focus and document the unexpected as you take the detour. Figure 6.1 can help you find your footing a bit faster as you make your initial plans. It might help you shift your stance without losing your balance when those plans go awry, too.

## Choosing and Using Tools and Platforms Responsibly

It's more important than ever to protect people's privacy, and I know that it's impossible for a child to truly understand and appreciate the complexities of consent. Seven-year-olds may feel comfortable sharing work that their twenty-something selves might refuse to. I'm constantly keeping this in mind. David Ulrich pushes my thinking even further here when he suggests that, as a collective, we're responsible for the way we use technology (Ulrich, 2018,

p. 188). We must always consider the potential unintended consequences of our choices and understand that, ultimately, technology should be used to deepen our humanity rather than diminishing it. I spend a great deal of time asking myself if my choices support that intention—especially in the age of artificial intelligence. You may be doing the same.

The purpose and practice of pedagogical documentation align with these values, but it's important to keep in mind that once we've shared images, recordings, and artifacts with others, we lose control over how they might use or share them. Unless we take care to investigate how privacy and data are protected within certain apps and on different platforms, sharing our data online is a risky endeavor. Keep this in mind as you choose the tools and platforms you use in your own documentation work.

> If you follow me on social media, then you know that I rarely share photos or images of the people I serve or their work. When I do, it's only after they (and if they are minors, their parents) have given me permission to do so. Even then, the images I share are often ten or more years old, and I still obscure each subject's face and often, the written content that I documented as I was learning from them.

Learning is a gloriously multimodal experience, and when we make learning visible, we express ourselves multimodally as well. We create visuals and arrange them in space. We speak our words, and we also put them down in print. We rely on sound, gesture, and even vibration to communicate our ideas to others. In order to document learning well, we need to use just-right tools. Photographs capture much that written words cannot. Video helps us document aspects of the same moment in a very different way. Audio recordings have their own distinct affordances. So do checklists and notebooks. So, how do we choose the best tool for any moment? And how do we use it well? Silvia Tolisano and Janet Hale (2018) suggest beginning with our learning goals and instructional plans (p. 91) and aligning our choices accordingly. Figure 6.1 illustrates my preferred tools and platforms, aligned to my specific documentation purposes. You'll find links to examples and some of my own reflective work in my digital documentation notebook as well.

## Agility Matters

When my plans and purposes shift unexpectedly, I often find myself switching up my tools in the moment too. This depends on how my subjects choose to make their learning visible. Sometimes, I've invited a specific type of expression that relies on a particular combination of modes. Planning to document learning is easier in these contexts, but even when I do this, there's no telling what learners will say, do, or create inside of any context, though. Those unpredictable moments are magic for most documentarians, and the more dynamic your tools, the more likely you'll be able to capture it, even when you're not quite sure what it means or how it might matter. I value my phone and tablets for this purpose, but paper works, too. If I can't take a photo, I can sketch or doodle an image. If I can't audio record, I can jot what I hear.

## Documenting the Learning, and Not Merely the Products of It

This is tricky, and it often takes practice to get there. When we're new and even marginally experienced documentarians, we often focus and capture products of learning rather than the learning itself. In my experience, this is complicated by our attention to learning goals and plans as well as assessments of mastery, which often have us thinking with the end in mind. It's also more efficient to document products of learning, and proof of mastery, and it's important to do so at times, too. This can also feel rewarding to new documentarians who aren't accustomed to making learning visible yet, let alone documenting it as it unfolds. Documenting products can feel gratifying because they're often complete, tidier, and seemingly detailed. They also invite us to check progress toward outcomes, and this is familiar territory for most teachers. When we document learning, images, recordings, and artifacts often demand a greater context in order to be understood. Those outside of the documentation experience—especially those who do not understand it—may look upon such evidence of learning with questioning and even skeptical eyes. What is that? They might wonder. What does it even mean? And how do we know? Interpretation helps us answer these questions—especially when we invite the subjects of our documentation work to inform our perspectives. We'll explore this with greater detail in Chapter 7.

## Processes and Postures

In my experience, documenting a learning moment often inspires me to capture others, and soon enough, I'm reflecting on the whole of a short journey. As I've explained before, sometimes those journeys turn into expeditions. But how do we know when it makes sense to expand a moment into a journey or an expedition? It's the recursive nature of pedagogical documentation that provides good answers here. As introduced in Chapter 1, you might remember that the process of documentation includes six distinct phases:

- ◆ Planning
- ◆ Making Learning Visible
- ◆ Observing
- ◆ Documenting Learning
- ◆ Interpreting the Data
- ◆ Inviting Diverse Perspectives

I typically move through this process once within any learning moment, but often, what I learn within that single moment motivates me to document another. My posture might change a bit from one experience to the next, and my purposes might as well—the kaleidoscope keeps tilting—but the process tends to remain the same whether I'm documenting a moment, a journey, or an expedition. Visit my digital documentation notebook to explore examples from my own practice that demonstrate this evolution. Notice how my posture and my purposes shift from one experience to another, even as the process remains the same. Consider how the discoveries made in one cycle inform the planning of the next.

Now, make an honest assessment of your current reality. I'll be honest: As a new documentarian, I was a careful planner. I was less experienced at making learning visible, although I often documented the results of it. I attempted to make meaningful observations, but I often felt my attention pulled in far too many directions. I wasn't very intentional about what I was trying to capture, and I struggled to make meaningful interpretations of the evidence I gathered. I rarely invited diverse perspectives, although I typically took care to invite my students to document and interpret their own learning for me. Any outsider looking in on my early work would question my purposes and notice countless weaknesses in my process. You might notice similar issues with your own work. This is because documentation isn't something we simply do. As I've mentioned previously, documentation is about becoming. We become documentarians. This happens over time, with deliberate practice, great reflection, and intentional goal setting. Figure 6.2 presents a learning progression for your own self-assessment and planning purposes. It's inspired by the work of Kenisha Bynoe and Angelique Thompson, the authors of *The Gift of Playful Learning: A Guide for Educators* (Thompson & Bynoe, 2023, p. 165). Their stories are shared throughout this text.

## Becoming a Documentarian: A Learning Progression

| Beginning | Approaching | Mastering | Evolving |
|---|---|---|---|
| Our plans are typically based upon needs identified by leaders.<br><br>We tend to study the products of learning, rather than the learning process.<br><br>We look and listen for evidence of knowledge and the mastery of skills.<br><br>We rely on written words, codes, checklists, and scoring tools to capture and reflect upon evidence of learning.<br><br>Data are assumed to be numbers and research is typically defined as quantitative.<br><br>Our interpretations of data are guided by a need to study performance and growth relative to competencies and standards that are defined by others.<br><br>These interpretations are often ours alone. | Our plans are driven by needs that we and other leaders have identified.<br><br>We are intentional about studying the process of learning and not merely its products.<br><br>We look and listen for evidence of learning that aligns to specific targets, goals, or purposes.<br><br>We begin capturing images and videos of what we see and audio recordings of what we hear.<br><br>Data and research are both qualitative and quantitative.<br><br>Our interpretations of the data are inspired by a desire to learn.<br><br>We invite colleagues and critical friends to interpret our data beside us. | Our plans are driven by needs and interests identified with our subjects in collaboration with leaders.<br><br>We're thoughtful about what constitutes learning and discriminating about what we document relative to it.<br><br>We capture evidence of learning that aligns to predetermined goals, but we also document and learn from the unexpected.<br><br>Learning stories are documented and shared multimodally. They're grounded in qualitative and quantitative data.<br><br>We invite our subjects, colleagues, critical friends, and others with diverse and necessary perspectives to inform our process and interpret findings.<br><br>These interpretations inform our next steps as documentarians. | Our plans shapeshift in response to the needs and interests of our subjects and other community members.<br><br>We shift between deductive and inductive postures with purpose, as we pursue meaningful questions about learners and learning.<br><br>Learning stories are multimodal, readily shared, accessible to all, and provocative. They inspire deeper and better questioning and documentation work.<br><br>Our subjects, colleagues, critical friends, and others with diverse perspectives challenge and change our plans, our thinking, our documentation practices and processes, and the theories that emerge from our work. |

*Figure 6.2—Becoming a Documentarian: A Learning Progression*

## Basic Moves for New Documentarians

In his 1980 book, *Camera Lucida*, Roland Barthes introduces his readers to two photography concepts: studium and punctum. The studium refers to the scene portrayed in the image. The details within the photograph that have the strongest emotional effect on the viewer are the punctum. These are the elements of an image that elicit a deep connection or resonance. They're the parts of the photo that move the viewer. These can be small details that catch the viewer's attention and leave a lasting impact. They may not necessarily be obvious or even centered in the frame. They can also leave the viewer feeling unsettled or even disturbed. When we consider the studium, we learn much about the photographer. The punctum, however, is conceived by the viewer. It's dependent on their identity, experience, and the knowledge they bring to image (Barthes, 1980).

While Barthes' theory attends specifically to the use of photography, contextualizing it across the whole of my documentation work has been grounding and clarifying. I offer the distinction to you with that intention, and if you're a beginner, then you might dedicate your first attempts to simply capturing the stadium—the scene. More experienced documentarians tend to think about the story they are trying to tell and the punctum, or the impact, they want their photograph, recording, or artifact to have. This is not to suggest that you can't go there right away if you're a beginner, but distinguishing studium from punctum can certainly help you scaffold your entry into this rich, complex work. Your early work doesn't have to be related to the classroom, your students, or what you're learning about them, either. You can practice inside of any context. Take some time documenting scenes of all kinds before you start tightening your aperture. Here are a few straightforward ways to begin:

◆ Choose a single setting. Commit to capturing a certain number of photos or recordings within a specific period of time. For instance, David Ulrich challenges photographers to take 100–200 photos a week while maintaining a loose and nonjudgmental process (Ulrich, 2018, p. 11). Your mileage may vary, but keep the number high enough to maintain a rapid, generative posture.

◆ You might begin by defining a concept or even a list of nouns or adjectives, and then take care to document them. Alternatively, you could take a scavenger hunt through the photo collections and videos you keep on your phone. Rather than documenting that single concept or capturing moments that represent those nouns or verbs you might simply notice them in the images and recordings you've already captured. You'll find an example of this in my documentation notebook.

◆ You might start with a simple question for your subjects, and then commit to audio or video recording their responses. A favorite: Where did you notice a shift in your mood today? Learners don't even have to explain why their mood changed, only when this happened. When I ask this question of myself or any group that participated in the same learning experience, their replies raise powerful questions. These questions are worth chasing further.

Once you've developed a comfort level capturing scenes using photo, audio, or video, you might make a simple attempt to annotate what you see or hear inside of any scene. There are many reasons to include annotation in your documentation toolkit. For instance, I find that there are some situations where pulling out my phone or inviting subjects to use their own devices disrupts the moment. When we begin documenting our learning, we shift from a learning posture to a documentation posture. Experienced documentarians ease into this adjustment comfortably, and many will tell you that they can maintain a foot in both worlds well—documentation is learning and all learning is somehow documented, perhaps. If you're a beginner though, know that it's not only okay for documentarians of all experience levels to leave the electronics tucked away sometimes because it's the better choice. Annotating what we see or hear is powerful stuff. Try these ideas, and visit my digital documentation notebook to see examples of them at work in my own world.

- ◆ Choose a color and look for it in a single setting. Tally the number of objects that carry it.
- ◆ Create a sociogram that illustrates how people in a setting communicate with one another. List all of the people gathered in your scene, and draw their interactions. Like this: Place the name of each person in a circle on a large sheet of paper or inside of a sketchbook. Then, add connections. For each interaction observed, draw a line from the initiator to the recipient. The end of the arrow should point to the person who is spoken to. If conversations are bidirectional, additional lines without arrows or double-headed arrows can be added.
- ◆ Capture shifts in your own mood as you observe a scene by doodling emojis. If it's useful, plot them in a way that makes these changes even more transparent.
- ◆ Visualize progress toward a learning target by sketching one inside of a notebook. Watch what learners do, and add dots to your illustration that represent how closely each of them has come to hitting that target. If you're ready, add notes about what you observed that supports this particular assessment.

## Growing through Experience

Once I'd committed to documenting my learning, it wasn't long before I grew dissatisfied with my practice. I'd become comfortable capturing a scene and specific elements within it. I'd learned some basic skills that supported meaningful interpretation. I'd even begun serving students who were documenting their own learning, and together, we were inviting people from beyond our small communities to offer diverse perspectives. I was ready to learn and do more and uncertain how to grow.

The experts that I'd followed within my own field were very generous with their own ideas, but when I made a broader study of pedagogical documentation, most of what I'd encountered was created for primary teachers alone. It was difficult to find documentarian friends who were learning besides older and more experienced writers, making that learning visible, and intentionally documenting their discoveries in some of the ways that this book attends to. That's why I want to introduce you to my friend Garreth Heidt and his student, Jane.

Garreth has been an important part of my learning network for quite some time now. I'm connected with him on LinkedIn and Twitter, where I have the privilege of learning from him as he engages with other educators who are interested in many of the same things both of us are: Enduring concepts and big ideas and the shapeshifting nature of teaching and learning. Garreth has always been one to push my thinking about design, multimodal composition, and pedagogical documentation. A committed documentarian himself, Garreth is the person who introduced me to Unrulr and Aaron Schorn. There are dozens of stories I could tuck into this text that would demonstrate Garreth's deep expertise here, but it's his recent exchange with a student named Jane that I found especially compelling.

As I write this chapter in July of 2023, I'm serving on an Artificial Intelligence working committee at my university. My colleagues and I are exploring the opportunities, challenges, and risks associated with AI, learning a great deal from educators and attorneys alike, and trying to establish a vision and policies that will serve learners and learning well. I'm documenting my learning about AI as I go, taking care to capture the process and not merely the products of this venture.

My conversations with Garreth and Jane have been essential here, and their willingness to share their documentation of their own related learning have been as well.

Here's the short story: In the spring of 2023, Garreth invited his students to do a bit of essaying. He distinguishes essay*ing* (the process of coherently composing a meaningful representation of evidence-based thought using varied expressive modes) from writing an essay (placing written words into that familiar five-paragraph frame). He'd already begun developing his students' awareness of AI, and so he wasn't surprised when a number of them submitted essays that lifted his suspicions.

Jane was one of those students, and Garreth had choices to make: He knew that he could have accused her of violating their shared commitment to academic integrity and offer no credit for her work. He could have contacted her parents and accused her of cheating. He could have assigned her in-school suspension or made an example of her in class. He could have made her the protagonist in some sad cautionary tale. He could have also reframed his instructional plans to try to beat the machine in the future.

Instead, he tried to learn more from Jane about why and how she used AI and what she discovered in the process.

And of course, that's what he did.

When I spoke with Jane this week, I was struck by how forthcoming and reflective she was. This is a young woman who is especially attuned to her learning, and I can't help but feel that Garreth created the conditions for this.

Beginners tend to use a wide aperture when they are documenting learning. They zoom out, capturing the whole of an entire scene. Meaningful documentation work demands discrimination though, and Jane was quite discriminating. She shared the whole of her experience for sure—explaining how excited she was to essay about Othello initially. She had a feminist theory to offer and planned to situate it within an uncommon treatment of the text. Each time she sat down to write, she willed the ideas to move out of her brain and across the screen, but they seemed to evaporate on the keyboard instead. Time grew tight, her anxiety got the best of her, and she turned to ChatGPT for a bit of assistance.

Still, she felt that the resulting essay was inhuman, and this isn't the first time a writer used that word to characterize AI-generated work. I asked if it failed to carry her voice and imprint, and she agreed that this was the case. I asked her if there were benefits to using AI, and she agreed that there certainly were. Her own experience handed her countless complexities to navigate, and so much important learning happened along the way.

And that's where our interview landed: squarely on the learning.

While Garreth could have punished Jane for using ChatGPT to write her essay, he chose to learn more from Jane about how AI can assist all of us in our essay*ing* instead. I rode in the sidecar as they began this journey together, and I've enjoyed great benefits along the way. Jane and Garreth made much of their learning visible to me as it unfolded. They shared artifacts of that learning, too.

Visit my digital documentation notebook to explore the whole of this story, from my unique perspective. Garreth and Jane each have their own as well, and I wonder how our truths might vary. So much of what we learn is dependent on our framing, tools, timing, and perspective. Experienced documentarians make choices about each of these essential elements that enable them to build their learning stories with intention. When the light bounces inside of any space and the tiles in our Documentation Kaleidoscope start tilting unexpectedly. As you gain more experience, your work with each of the following essential elements, adapted from Latz (2017), may become more complex.

◆ Framing: Moments will begin expanding into journeys more often, and you may find yourself pursuing questions and themes that were informed by previous experiences. As you consider what's worth documenting in each new moment, you may begin to realize that documentation is sharpening your thinking, refining your questions, and changing the way you frame the learning you're capturing. As a beginner, you may have asked yourself, "What's essential to document in this lesson?" Experienced documentarians are even more thoughtful about considering why. New documentarians ask, "What learning should be made visible within this specific scene?" Those with experience also wonder, "To what degree should we make learning visible?" and "Which modes of expression and which tools will enable us to capture this learning in a just-right way?" New documentarians define what will be included in their documentation. Experienced documentarians also consider what won't be. The decisions we make are unique to us. We each have a distinct way of defining our academic, intellectual, or even emotional focus (Ulrich, 2018, p. 27).

◆ Tools: You will likely realize that your use of tools becomes increasingly dynamic as you strive to capture the most complete version of any story that unfolds. Each mode of expression affords learners something that others do not, and as they strive to make their thinking visible, many mix modes in order to demonstrate what they need to in a just-right way. The tools we use possess their own affordances as well, and as you gain experience as a documentarian, you may find yourself dissatisfied with the approaches you've leaned on heavily as a beginner. You'll be eager to expand your repertoire, and I hope that all of the tools I've tucked into this text, it's appendix, and my digital documentation notebook serve you well as you grow.

> **?** What if you can't afford expensive tools? Documenting your learning doesn't require their use. Consider using low-tech approaches like inviting learners to complete written reflections, or by capturing annotations when you confer with them. Encourage them to draw or build their processes. Make notes. Preserve your primary sources. Ask colleagues, parents, and other community members to donate discarded phones so that you might use their cameras. Repurpose other donated tools as well. Allow children to bring their own devices to class. Let them use their cell phones to capture learning made visible.

◆ Point of view: How will you focus your head, your heart, your eyes, and your ears upon the scene? Our documentation efforts are the direct result of our experiences, expertise, and identities. New documentarians tend to use them as lenses through which they steady their gaze. Experienced documentarians know that who they are and where they come from might cloud or even corrupt their vision, though. They realize it's subjective and that in fact, our observations are never neutral (Dahlberg, 2012, p. 225). We need to take care to assume responsibility here. Documentation isn't about perceiving reality—it's about constructing it. When we center the voices of those we're documenting in the work, we invite them to co-create that reality with us. We also serve them in their efforts to document and deepen their own learning. Each documentarian can only capture the learning as they see it. Their stories only reveal the truth as they know it. Visit my digital documentation notebook to learn more about how I access and learn from the voices of the subjects I serve.

◆ Timing: As a new documentarian, I often timed my work by thinking about where within a specific event I would take care to make learning visible, in order to capture it. Now, the questions I'm chasing often enter my dreams, as I'm sleeping. They follow me around my garden as I'm tending my plants. They pop up in dinner conversations with friends who share my passion for teaching writing. These questions of mine are worth pursuing because their answers will help me understand and serve learners better, and because of this, I find that they've already shaped who I am, what I do, and how I do it. I no longer have to orchestrate moments or go to great lengths to make thinking visible. Experienced documentarians often tell me the same. They teach in a documentation-friendly manner every day now. This gives them more time to consider the quality of the prompts and protocols they use, how they will situate them within a learning moment, and their pacing as documentarians of learning.

*When I asked Lisa to tell me about her growth as a documentarian, she spoke about how much more discriminating she became about what she was documenting and when and how. As I explained before, Lisa began documenting for a very distinct purpose early on: She was eager to capture evidence of her student's progress toward specific literacy outcomes. Over time, she became very skilled—even strategic—in this work, though. She developed efficient annotation systems, and she began noticing that because her practice was habitual, her focus was far sharper. She noticed things quickly, interpreted them on her feet, and used what she was learning to determine her next steps, almost rhythmically. Suddenly, she found herself asking better and more specific questions about what she was seeing and hearing. She was following up with her students, inquiring more, and seeking their perspectives, too.*

*"I never planned to start documenting learning in every subject area, but that's what ended up happening," she laughed with me, as I interviewed her for this book in the spring of 2023. "And it's made me so happy in my work. The kids just amaze me. Documentation is helping me become the teacher I've always wanted and knew I could become."*

*This struck me because it's how I feel about my own experience with documentation as well. In fact, many of the people that I interviewed for this book and even my own students have spoken to the effect of documentation on the development of their identities, the deepening of their self-awareness, and their enthusiasm for this work. I wrote this book for you because I know that pedagogical documentation saved me from burnout at least a thousand times and maybe more. It's helped me negotiate many tensions in my work and in the field of literacy instruction as well. Documentation is grounding, giving, and generative work. Lisa understands this, and I hope that your experiences are just as meaningful for you, no matter how messy they might become.*

## Frozen in Amber

Amber is a hardened, translucent substance that forms over millions of years from the resin of ancient trees. When a tree is damaged, it secretes resin as a defense mechanism, which can then trap small organisms such as insects, spiders, or plant material. Over time, the resin hardens and fossilizes, preserving the trapped organisms in remarkable detail. These amber fossils have provided scientists with valuable insights into ancient ecosystems and the evolution of various species.

The concept of being "frozen in amber" entered popular culture through the literary work of Michael Crichton. In his 1993 novel, *Jurassic Park*, Crichton introduced the idea of extracting dinosaur DNA from mosquitoes trapped in amber. The fictional portrayal of mosquitoes preserved in amber with intact dinosaur blood led to the idea that ancient creatures or even entire ecosystems could be resurrected through the discovery of well-preserved specimens.

As an experienced documentarian, I worry that my data—the images and recordings and artifacts I collect—fix learners and learning in time, deluding me into conclusions that are only briefly relevant or worse—corrupted by the kind of nostalgia that does great harm. Our projects become our darlings. I know this. As I've mentioned before, each of us brings our distinct identities to this work as well. How we orient ourselves within a project shifts over time, in response to how it, and we unfold. This happens within a moment, inside of a journey, and across the whole of every lengthy documentation expedition. This is why curate learning moments in a variety of ways and more importantly—it's why I strive to keep these data loose. It's important to remember that moments pass, journey's end, and expeditions carry us down wildly different paths. Documentation projects end, but the learning that began in that moment continues, and it changes us. Often, it changes the conclusions we once drew, too.

When we keep our data loose, we're able to lift it out of one context—one project—and place it within another. What we capture becomes a source of our previous experiences and learning that we can carry into entirely different documentation contexts and projects. In my opinion, this is the greatest gift of the digital documentation age. My data lives inside of folders that invite me to mix, remix, see, and re-see what happened and what it means as I learn, grow, and come to know people who are very different from those who were involved in that recorded learning moment. When I bring documentation from a previous project completed with one community of learners into another, it changes how we think and work in the present. It also helps me reflect on the past. Sometimes, I'm able to bring the subjects from one project into the spaces where new projects are unfolding. Imagine the exponential learning that happens in situations like these. I've shared some of those stories in my digital documentation notebook, beside strategies and tools that can help you keep your own data loose.

**TLDR (Too Long, Didn't Read)**

1. Newer documentarians might want to take a deductive approach as they study learning within a single moment. For example, documenting your learning about how a new instructional strategy influences learners in a single lesson.
2. Documenting a single moment may raise questions that inspire a shift in posture. We might begin in a deductive stance and find ourselves shifting to an inductive one, and vice versa.
3. Often, documentation plans don't go as planned. Take the detour. It likely isn't a failure but will instead lead to better learning and outcomes.
4. Choose your documentation tools with intention. What are you observing? When? Where? Which tools will help you capture this learning best?
5. Agility matters because learning is messy. Prepare to be disrupted.

6. Remember to document the learning, and not just the products of it.
7. Our framing, tools, points of view, and timing will shift as we gain experience as documentarians. Expect this.
8. When we keep our data loose, we're better able to recontextualize it as we learn and do more, too.

### Let's Reflect

Which parts of the documentation process do you feel prepared to navigate? Where are you less certain? Why? How will you resolve this tension? Refer to the appendix and my digital documentation notebook if you're seeking inspiration, examples, or potential solutions.

### Try This: Just Right Tools and Invitations

Document a moment, and really focus on capturing the learning, scene-by-scene, rather than the products of learning.

Or, document a journey and then ask yourself, "How might I use the tools and ideas shared in this text to better mitigate my own biases?"

Or explore documentation gathered over an entire expedition. Examine how the frames and tools you used, the points of view you took, and your timing influenced the work. What was helpful? What would you do differently?

## References

Barthes, R. (1980). *Camera lucida: Reflections on photography*. Hill and Wang, a division of Farrar, Straus and Giroux.

Crichton, M. (1993). *Jurassic Park*. Arrow.

Dahlberg, G. (2012). Pedagogical documentation: A practice for negotiation and democracy. In C. Edwards, L. Gandini, & G. Forman (Eds.), *The hundred languages of children: The Reggio Emilia experience in transformation* (3rd ed., pp. 225–232). Praeger.

Latz, A. O. (2017). *Photovoice research in education and beyond: A practical guide from theory to exhibition*. Routledge, Taylor & Francis Group.

Tolisano, S. R., & Hale, J. A. (2018). *A guide to documenting learning: Making thinking visible, meaningful, shareable, and amplified*. Corwin.

Thompson, A., & Bynoe, N. K. (2023). *The gift of playful learning: A guide for educators*. Shell Education Publishing.

Ulrich, D. (2018). *Zen camera: Creative awakening with daily practice in photography*. Watson-Guptill.

Vance, J. [@jess_vanceedu]. (2023, February 12). "How to build a learning wall: A four point checklist." [Photographs]. https://www.instagram.com/p/CokhP9fORze/?utm_source=ig_web_copy_link&igshid=MzRlODBiNWFlZA==

# 7

# How Will You Interpret Your Data?

As I draft this chapter in the spring of 2023, there's a war raging on Twitter, in the tab right next to this one, and if I click into it, I know I'll never meet this morning's word count. Whenever I wander that battlefield, I see friends on both sides. In another life—the before times—I would have stopped to wave. I would have called them over to have a peek at something that was coming up in my own learning or work. I would have asked their perspective or inquired about what they were reading these days. But I've learned not to ask too many questions on Twitter anymore, and that saddens me.

Once upon a time, it was a place I couldn't wait to visit before or after work began each day. Maybe you remember how, in the beginning, those of us who wanted to be of use spent hours curating and sharing resources and tools there each week until the stream began churning so hard and moving so fast that none of us could keep up anymore. We were all so eager to soak up the best of the web and then pour it back into the learning networks we'd established there. We wanted to learn everything that we could. Make a difference. Find our people. And we did. I guess we still do behind cover, as we wait on some sort of ceasefire.

I'm not sure that I ever felt called to battle, but I've watched people that I admire taking and then returning heat. I've watched this war change them and the entire face of a virtual landscape that I once thought of as my personal professional learning community. I understand why these tensions over reading instruction exist. Here's where I struggle, though: I'm not confident that many of the most decorated soldiers in this war ever document their learning or invite their students to. And if they do, I'm not certain that their work is as textured

DOI: 10.4324/9781003333241-10

and nuanced as it needs to be. If it were, they would be less angry because they'd be less certain about their points of view. They'd also be too dedicated to their own learning to devote this much time to shaming and blaming others.

As I've explained, those who practice deductive documentation study learning in order to test the theories that others have developed. They lift that theory out of a book, an article, or a professional learning experience, situate it inside of their own unit or lesson or interaction with students, and then they document the learning that's made visible. Their interpretations help them understand its fit.

I remember how, as a young middle school teacher, my friend Kristen Marchiole and I would sit on the porch in the summer and co-plan lessons for the following year. When school began, we shifted our meetings to the classroom, where we met before our students arrived or during lunch most days. Our district invested a great deal in us, and we were committed to implementing the best practices that we'd only begun learning about: cooperative learning, differentiated instruction, and promising co-teaching strategies. I remember how, a few years into our work together, we wondered aloud about how we were embracing our learning, appreciating the way each new practice was changing how we were teaching for the better, and why some colleagues weren't having the same results and sharing their grievances about that rather loudly.

"It's because we keep trying," Kristen said. "We aren't just throwing some new strategy into a lesson and then giving up on it when it doesn't seem to work."

"We keep tinkering until we make it work," I nodded, reflecting beside her and realizing for perhaps the first time that I'd found a learning partner and that our efforts to get things right were making us fast friends. It was also helping us fall in love with teaching all over again. No one referred to what we were doing as documentation back then, but when I think about how we approached our work. I consider the intentionality behind each lesson, the focal point we created, and the way we invited our students to make their learning visible and talk with us about their processes and practices and the why behind their choices. I can't help but see how even then, pieces of this now essential practice were already engaging and sustaining us.

> If you're able, consider recording your planning meetings on Zoom. Use this documentation to analyze your learning and growth and the quality of your collaborative efforts over time. If I could return to the days whenKristen and I were planning together, I would do this. We were fortunate to have great support for early co-teaching efforts and administrators who knew we needed deep and sustained professional learning in order to do our very best work together. Imagine if we'd documented it well. Imagine if we'd recorded those meetings. I wish I could view them today.

We were committed to kidwatching, holding onto the discoveries we made each day, and then making dedicated time during each week to sit with one another and interpret the findings (Goodman & Owocki, 2002). The more we learned and the more reflective we became together, the less certain we grew about the conclusions we were drawing. Oddly enough, our instruction became far more impactful, though. This taught me, early on, that the way to find out which practices are truly "best" is to document my learning and invite my students to do the same as we begin testing them, and then refining our practices over time. Capturing the photographs, recordings, and artifacts of learning is just a piece of what it means to do this well, though. It's how we make meaning from these data that opens a world of new understandings and potential as we strive to remember, understand, and be of better service to others.

## Analytic Memos Offer a Simple Start

Analytic memos are reflections that you compose throughout the documentation process. They capture your thinking about what you're observing and hearing, the data you're collecting, and what it might mean. Most of my analytic memos live on sticky notes that I tuck into my sketchbooks or plans. They summarize my processes, name what I'm noticing in the data I'm capturing, and help me tease out concepts or themes that are emerging in my work. As I gain more experience as a documentarian, my analytic memos contain questions, too. They inspire me to gather new and different data. They help me imagine the next moment I will document and the thinking I might want to make visible within it. As I prepared to write this book, I combed through dozens of my documentation notebooks, sketchbooks, and collections of sticky notes. I can tell you with confidence that analytic notes are a primary form of documentation for me. You'll find examples in my digital documentation notebook.

If you're a new documentarian, entering a learning moment with a question that inspires this kind of reflection is a simple way to begin shifting between documenting learning and interpreting the evidence of it yourself. You might pause to wonder:

- What am I seeing in the data I'm collecting?
- What did I think I would see that is actually missing?
- What did I think I would hear, and what am I actually hearing in my recordings?
- How does what I'm seeing relate to what I'm hearing?
- What does my documentation seem to center on: people, practices, processes, places, or products of learning? What does this reveal

about my intended or unintended purposes? What does it reveal about my perspective?

◆ What questions arise from this work?

◆ Which concepts am I tracing across multiple data points?

◆ What theories are beginning to emerge?

◆ Whose voices are missing as I make this interpretation, and how might I access them?

◆ How is my perspective limited, and whose interpretation might expand it?

These questions that you carry into your classroom become lenses that can help you make meaning from your data after the active learning moment has passed and you're fully immersed in interpreting it.

You may appreciate this as well: As I continue processing images and recordings captured long ago, these same questions are helping me bring new and better-informed eyes to that early learning and documentation work. I find that they're simple but profound, if I'm patient in my processing. They made for productive documentation experiences when I was new and uncertain in my practice. They're deepening it now, as those early moments have expanded into journeys and expeditions. You'll find additional tools and protocols that support your first attempts at interpretation in the appendix.

## Deepening Your Practice

My first attempts to employ grounded theory methodologies were sadly unscientific, highly experimental, and profoundly transformational. While this text will not take a deep dive into that process, there are elements of it that are worth sharing here, and I encourage you to learn more about it in my digital documentation notebook. When documentarians adopt this approach, they ground the theories they create in the lived learning experiences of those they serve, rather than replicating or testing those already developed by experts in their chosen field.

Although grounded theory was first developed by sociologists Barney Glaser and Anselm Strauss in the 1960s, it has evolved over time in response to what's been learned through application. Rather than beginning with a preconceived theory, researchers rely on the data they collect to develop theories of their own. While many practitioners assert that the theories emerge from the data, more contemporary academics emphasize the role of interpretation in the conclusions that emerge.

> ❓ "How do I take care to mitigate bias and prevent harm to others as a documentarian?"
>
> Bias is inherent in all of our work, and as a documentarian, the threats it may pose are even higher. It's important to maintain this awareness, speak to this reality, and remain humble when sharing any theories that emerge from your work. Be clear about your own identity, your role, and your positionality when you speak to your work. Use multiple measures of assessment, and gather the best critical friends around you if you're considering sharing your findings widely. I also find it important to make as much of my work open-source as possible. I invite teachers who are very different from me to test my ideas with learners who are very different from the children I teach. I don't do this in order to suggest that my ideas are in any way best practices. Quite the opposite. I make my work open source and invite wide applications of it in an effort to further mitigate bias and receive feedback from a diverse group of users.

For instance, Anselm Strauss and Juliet Corbin, in their 1990 publication *"Basics of Qualitative Research: Grounded Theory Procedures and Techniques,"* suggest an alternative approach to grounded theory than the original version proposed by Glaser and Strauss. They argue that the data alone do not generate theory, but instead, the interpretative work of the researcher is essential.

This acknowledges the constructivist nature of the research process. Constructivist grounded theory, developed by Kathy Charmaz, emphasizes that researchers bring their own perspectives, experiences, and interactions to the process of developing a grounded theory. In Charmaz's view, grounded theories are not discovered within the data, but are constructed by researchers through their engagement with the data.

These perspectives contrast with Glaser's more purist view, which holds that grounded theories should emerge from the data with minimal interpretive intervention from the researcher. This reflects a key debate within grounded theory—and qualitative research more generally—about the nature of knowledge, the role of the researcher, and the relationship between data and theory (Latz, 2017, pp. 95–96).

This was helpful for me to know, and it's something I take care to remember each time I bring the theories that have emerged from my own work into spaces where others might embrace them. When I wrote my first book, I took care to explain the experimental nature of my work and the uncertainty I maintained about the theories that I was sharing. Over the years, I've reminded audiences that I work with in any setting that what I'm discovering and sharing about teaching writing well is the result of my own documentation work and those projects that others are pursuing as a result of what I've shared. It's my strong belief that inquiry-based professional learning is essential to building and sustaining our profession, our relationships with one another, and the kinds of cultures that will ultimately serve learners well.

This is how we end the war—by having enough humility to admit that we're all still learners, despite our growing expertise.

If you're an experienced documentarian who is interested in deepening your practice, you might appreciate practicing elements of grounded theory as well. And I use the word practicing with great intention here. I'm not an expert, but I learn much from those who are. You may want to try my modified approach, explained here. You'll find case studies that speak to it in my digital documentation notebook, besides images that can help you visualize and perhaps replicate my efforts. There, you'll see how my experiences with coding have deepened. The appendix links you to some of my favorite resources here.

1.  **Document Your Learning:** Define your vision, your purposes for documentation, and the context through which your efforts will be made. Plan to make learning visible, as I've described in earlier chapters of this book, and then use the tools at your disposal to document your learning.

2.  **Display Your Data:** After the moment has passed, create a display of your data. When I'm working with images, I typically print them and then spread them across a large table. When I've audio-recorded interviews or conferences, I take care to print the transcripts. When I video record, I do the same, but I also add notes that refer to the subjects' facial expressions, gestures, and other body language as well as descriptions of the setting, important artifacts included in the recording, and movement across space. If I'm working with artifacts, I spread the original items or images of them across a table as well. Visit my documentation notebook to view images of what this phase of my process has looked like in the past.

3.  **Engage in Open Coding:** Once you've created your display, begin analyzing each bit of data individually. If you're reviewing written words, take them line-by-line. If you're viewing photos, zoom in and even segment them. Study one element of the image at a time. Look for patterns in the emerging concepts you notice. Create clusters of data that reveal common themes. Identify your most robust clusters. Establish a category for each of them, and keep those less significant data groups close as well. They may matter over time.

4. **Begin Axial Coding:** Notice the relationships between categories. Questions like these may be useful: What is the relationship between x and y? If you change x, how might it impact y? How does x enhance y? How does x diminish y? What does x require of y? What does x afford the learner or learning that y does not? What would be lost or gained if we removed x from y? When we vary x, how does it alter y? How is x tempered by y? What is the effect of x and y on z? (Stockman, 2022).

5. **Shift to Selective Coding:** At this point in your inquiry, you will likely begin shaping a few working theories, almost intuitively. You may find yourself combining and refining your categories, integrating your findings, and being compelled by new questions that inspire another round of documentation.

6. **Begin Theoretical Coding:** Now, you will begin to document additional learning moments in response to what you've noticed so far and what you continue to wonder.

7. **Memo Writing:** Analytic memos play an important role in this process as well. As your inquiry work unfolds, take care to make notes that capture your reflections on the process and your discoveries, new curiosities, and questions worth pursuing in your next round of documentation.

## Seeking Diverse Perspectives

I remember when a writer I'll refer to as Maria began using sticky notes to organize and then tinker with the structure of a story she was writing. I was seated at my desk in my writing studio, conferring with another writer, when she approached us to ask if she could use our whiteboard.

"Sure," I replied, a bit surprised by the ask. Most writers chose to sit at tables or sprawl comfortably across beanbag chairs or on the floor. Maria assumed a position in front of our large dry-erase board and began spreading sticky notes across it. As my conversation with the writer seated beside me came to a close, I turned my attention to what she was doing, and then I took a picture. You'll find it in my digital documentation notebook, beside the analytical notes I captured on that day and sometime afterward, too.

This was an unexpected learning moment, and the quality of that image reveals how I was caught off-guard. It's grainy, the lighting is bad, and no viewer can see the content of those notes. Still, there is much to consider in that powerful data point, as you will see in my digital documentation notebook. Weeks later, as I was telling a colleague about Maria's approach, the writer herself overheard me celebrating her.

"The way she was using her sticky notes to plan and then restructure her story was just brilliant," I remember gushing. "I'm glad she did it so publicly—others were watching, and now a few of them are benefiting from Maria's invention. They're telling me it helps."

"That's not what happened," Maria admitted quietly shortly after this exchange and much to my confusion. "I didn't invent that strategy. You did. Don't you remember? You were playing with sticky notes in kind of the same way a while back. I was just doing what you already did at first, and then I added a few ideas of my own to the process." I hadn't remembered, I admitted. And how gracious of her to correct me, I added.

This wasn't the only time that my memory of an event is a reflection of history as I alone remember it. This wasn't the only time that my enthusiasm for an idea or a perspective that I alone am taking clouds my recollections and the interpretations I'm making of any data I've collected. This example that I've shared about my experience with Maria is a simple one that prompts a far more powerful point: We all bring our own experiences, identities, and biases to the interpretation of our data, and our theories emerge from that. The most important perspective you need to seek is the perspective of the learners you are serving and the people whose processes, practices, and work are the subjects of your investigation. You'll also need critical friends.

---

Critical friends push us to self-reflect, rethink our positions, and improve the theories we're creating. They illuminate our biases, challenge the status quo, and facilitate open and honest discussions about the problems and opportunities that any documentation project offers us. The best critical friends are typically external to our work, and they bring fresh eyes and uncommon perspectives to the process. Where might you find the best critical friends for your documentation project? Make a list. Keep adding to it.

---

Finding critical friends can be challenging if you haven't had the opportunity to establish or grow your own learning network. I rely on my own heavily here, and this is why, as social media continues to evolve in unpredictable ways, I take care to maintain my relationships with the colleagues I've met inside of social learning spaces who push my thinking the most. If you're in need of a critical friend, I hope you'll reach out to me. I may not be the right fit for your project, but I'm glad to introduce you to others who may be. You might consider approaching administrators, mentors, and teacher leaders on your campus as well. Inviting local colleagues and those across the distance to join a critical friends group may be worthwhile if you're committed to sustaining your documentation efforts. Publishing my work is my ongoing attempt to invite critical friendships as well. Everything I share is still a work in progress, when readers encounter my ideas, they often test them in their own contexts, too. Then, they drop me messages by email or through our social learning spaces, offering their reflections, asking good questions, and shifting my perspectives in small and more significant ways. This has made me more self-aware and improved my practice, too.

These are often uncomfortable experiences that humble me. Hard. This is a necessary part of learning though, and it's absolutely essential for those of us who are straight, cis-gendered, white, and privileged. If this is you, it's important to ask yourself which critical friends are keeping you conscious of your power and positionality. Which critical friends are ensuring that you're sensitive to your own biases? Which will hold you accountable for the theories you create and share? Who is helping you understand that it's your impact and not your intentions that matter most? If you don't have answers, please reach out. I'm glad to problem-solve with you.

## Co-Constructing Meaning

When we invite others to interpret our data beside us or even in contexts where we aren't present, we mitigate our own bias and benefit from the collective experiences and expertise of every participant. Seeking their diverse perspectives often changes our own. Even when they validate or own emerging theories or echo the same questions we're teasing out of our analyses, we're bettered by having company. Our projects and the conclusions we draw from them are no longer ours alone. As you plan to invite others to interpret your data with you, questions like these are helpful:

- ◆ Who are these data about, and how might I invite their perspectives?
- ◆ Why will I invite their perspectives?
- ◆ When will I bring them into the work: As I'm planning, during the active learning moment, in the wake of it, or once I've displayed my data?
- ◆ How will I share my data?
- ◆ How will I invite them to work with it?
- ◆ When will I share my own interpretations with them?
- ◆ How might we co-construct meaning?

The third part of this book can help you envision, design, and move through your own documentation projects with a bit of guidance and good company. Invitations to reflect and construct purposeful responses to each of these questions are offered there, besides tools and protocols that will help you step into this work. I should add this here, though: Nothing about documentation moves in a straight line. This is reflexive work that constantly brings us back to where we began, inviting us to reflect upon and even interrogate our purposes, approaches, assumptions, and conclusions. Learning is complex, and so are people and the interactions we share. As an inexperienced documentarian, this often overwhelmed me. I assumed that because I couldn't capture or study the whole of any learning moment the work was somehow inadequate and I was failing. As an experienced documentarian, my perspective is very different now. I know that I won't be able to capture the whole of any learning moment. The work is inadequate, and I am humbled by this. I remain committed to learning, sharing, seeking diverse perspectives, and inviting others to test the theories that are emerging from my own work so that we might collaborate together. The only failure is in refusing to learn.

*Aaron Schorn finds that people of all ages are far more likely to document their learning when there is a purpose and they know someone's going to see it. I've spent some time reflecting on this statement ever since he first shared it, mostly within the context of my own work. I'll be honest: There are few educators that I connect with in my daily life who are truly enthusiastic about the things I love to learn about. I'm passionate about multimodal composition and the influence of assessment on student motivation. I'm into competency-based learning and especially multiliteracies, and I know very well that if I bring any of these things up over dinner with family or friends their eyes will quickly glaze over. That's one of the reasons why I began building and still work so hard to sustain a professional learning network online. I've found my teacher-friends there. And now, I document my learning so that I can make it more transparent and accessible for them. They do the same for me. We're colleagues, bound together by the way we document and share our learning. So I have to agree: I'm more likely to document when I have a purpose, and the fact that my network is looking forward to what I share makes the work even more thrilling to me.*

There are many ways to share our data with others in a way that invites their perspective. I'll mention again that our choices must be sensitive to the needs and interests of our subjects. We need to gain their consent to share, and even when they offer it, we need to take good care to protect their privacy. These are a few of the steps I take to better ensure this:

- ◆ I share my intentions and purposes openly and early in our relationship.
- ◆ I promise that any images, videos, or artifacts that I gather will not be shared without their consent.
- ◆ I ask them, their parents, and their guardians to complete a general release. You'll find examples in the appendix.
- ◆ I de-identify them from the data unless doing so violates their best interests or compromises the quality of our learning or work.

    – I ascribe symbols to participants and rely on them rather than requiring the capture and display of their names.
    – I avoid capturing learners' faces in images and video recordings whenever possible.
    – I blur faces when sharing images that don't rely on facial expression for meaning.
    – When I share data online, it's typically 8–10 years old or more. The subjects have grown. Many live in different places.

- ◆ When I do share their images, videos that offer a complete portrait of who they are, lengthy audio recordings, or samples of their work, I invite them into the environments I'm doing this within, I share recordings of those meetings if they aren't able to attend, and I ensure that their voices are elevated and their contributions are seen for what they are: Invaluable expertise that contributes to our learning. The subjects of our documentation projects are the experts we seek and learn most from. It's important that they are positioned this way in the work.

## Building and Working a Display

As a new documentarian, I devoted a great deal of time to capturing just-right data. This is the focus of a good portion of this book, and it makes sense that we take good care here. As I've mentioned before, moments are fleeting. We can't return to them once they've passed, and being thoughtful about what we will try to document, when, and how is important. Documentation doesn't end when the learning moment is over, though. In many ways, it's only just beginning. Displaying our data helps us make better meaning from it initially and deepen that meaning over time.

There are many ways to display data, and you'll find additional recommendations in the appendix. These are the approaches that I find most useful, though. They're the ones that have had the most profound influence on my own work.

## Documentation Notebooks

I began toting a sketchbook around with me each day somewhere around 2010. It was a place to drop sticky notes—the tools I use most often as I'm wandering a room, peeking over shoulders, and talking with young writers. Sticky notes enable me to jot quick observations or reflections that remain loose and moveable, and this matters. Analysis challenges us to mix and remix our data. When we capture them bit-by-bit, it facilitates this work.

The way I use my sketchbooks has evolved over time, as I've worked with them. They've become multimedia documentation notebooks that capture and enable me to make and remake meaning day-by-day and then season-by-season. This has been one of the most rewarding things about using them—the way they've taught me how to use them. These are just a few ways that a documentation notebook might serve you. I'd love to know more about how your mileage varies if this is your practice, too. Come find me on social media to chat more, if you'd like:

◆ I use my documentation notebook to store the notes I capture as I'm observing and learning inside of any moment. I don't walk the room with it in hand, but I do have sticky notes and my phone with me. I scribble observations on the notes, snap photos, record videos, and then dump it all into my sketchbook rather haphazardly at first. I love printing $2 \times 2$ images on single sheets of paper and then cutting them apart and using painter's tape to secure them to sketchbook pages. Painter's tape allows me to remove and reposition the images in different configurations as I move through my analyses. More on that below.

◆ I use my notebook to notice and name the ideas, concepts, and patterns I see within and across different data points. I scribble these reflections in the margins.

◆ I begin theorizing here, too. Some pages of my sketchbook are devoted to lengthy written reflections that inspire me to teach differently or better, rework a theory, or design a new resource or tool. As I'm drafting this manuscript, I'm returning to single sketchbook pages that capture my learning within a single moment, entire books that house my documentation work and reflections over the course of a journey. This book you hold in your hands is the result of a career-long expedition. It's been something revisiting all of my sketchbooks in order to create this manuscript for you.

◆ I leave my documentation notebooks on tables in some of the rooms I teach and learn within so that the people I'm serving—whether they're grown adults or children—might leaf through the pages, leave their own notes, and push my thinking around what they're seeing there.

◆ I also build shared notebooks inside the communities I serve within, too. Sometimes, I'll invite young writers to create individual pages, and we add them to a shared notebook. I'll ask teachers to contribute in a similar way as well. This is particularly powerful when we're engaged in purposeful inquiry work around a shared priority. It's been my experience that this plays an important role in improving learning outcomes for students. Each time that I'm asked to assist English teachers in boosting performance, we typically use varied data to develop hunches about how we might intervene. Concepts live inside of these theories, and it can be very helpful to invite teachers to go looking for them in their own classrooms and practice. Each creates a page, and when we put them together, we begin to notice how our interpretations and treatments of these concepts align and deviate. We begin to build a portrait of our current reality. Documentation notebooks help us study our evolution over time as well. These data matter. If this interests you, you'll find case studies that make the process more explicit in my digital documentation notebook.

*"When I saw your sketchbook, it made me want to start keeping one of my own," Lisa tells me as she lifts her own copy up to her camera so I can see it on my side of the screen. It's not the first time I've had a peek at it, and like Lisa, I tend to swoon whenever I am able to meander the pages of anyone's documentation notebook. They're often a multimodal mosaic of learning that awakens the senses and creates deep curiosity.*

*Lisa's annotation system strikes me initially. I appreciate how she documents learner progress toward her goals and outcomes. It's the reflections in the margins of her sketchbook that move me most, though. This is where her thinking about those data is revealed, and I find it breathtaking.*

*Lisa's sketchbook is a place where she is becoming far more intentional about her teaching. I notice the alignment between her learning intentions, the success criteria she's established for them, and students' progress toward them. More importantly, I notice her evaluating the decisions she's making in the margins. I notice her studying, as John Hattie would suggest, her impact (Hattie, 2023, pp. 308–309). This, more than anything else, is what makes pedagogical documentation a powerful instructional tool. Drop into my digital documentation notebook to have a peek at a few pages of Lisa's sketchbook, if you'd like.*

## Documentation Panels

I'm a Reggio-inspired documentarian. By this, I mean that my approach is heavily influenced by the mid-nineteenth-century Italian women from the province of Reggio Emilia, Italy, who worked beside theorist Loris Malaguzzi to conceptualize an instructional approach that recognizes the inherent abilities and rights of all children. Dr. Carlina Rinaldi and the pedagogistas who honor and sustain their legacy rely on pedagogical documentation to inform and shape their thinking (Rinaldi, 2021). I've completed several study tours there, and my last invited a much deeper exploration of pedagogical documentation, including their use of documentation panels: visual archives of learning that include images, artifacts, documents, and written reflections.

Early examples of this work include large panels like those you see in Figure 7.1. Constructed primarily by teachers, documentation panels tell the story of a learning moment, journey, or expedition. Typically built on walls, contemporary examples have gone digital, and invited rich collaboration between students, teachers, and other learning partners who interpret the data and offer diverse perspectives.

I've always been hesitant to share the documentation panels that I've constructed with teachers and learners because they're often pretty, and as I've learned, pretty threatens to undermine our learning about pedagogy. Our brains love beautiful things, and any Reggio-inspired instructor will tell you that aesthetic matters. Documentation panels are often gorgeous, but as Dr. Diane Kashin reminds us, designing and interpreting the display with intention is the most essential work if we're eager to use what we learn about and from students to improve the learning and work that we do. In other words, we must take care to build and then make a meaningful interpretation of each display (Kashin, 2016).

There are many ways to accomplish this of course, and I share different thoughts and challenges in my documentation notebook, but in preparing this manuscript for publication, I made a study of the approaches I've relied upon most

*Figure 7.1—An Example of a Documentation Panel*

often, and affinity mapping showed up in my own practice and again. Here's how you might use it to build and work a documentation panel of your own:

- ◆ Make and capture meaningful observations of learners.
- ◆ Post up your findings. If you're creating a physical documentation panel, you'll do this on a wall or any other large, empty space.
- ◆ Review your data and begin to create affinities: Cluster images, artifacts, documents, and reflections together if they seem relevant to the same question, concept, or idea.
- ◆ Define what these data help you notice—alone and together. Consider the questions they raise. Use protocols like the one you see in Figure X to interpret these data further.
- ◆ Use what you learn to create, and then plan to test new theories relevant to learners and learning, teachers and teaching. Explore a variety of use cases specific to documentation panels in my digital documentation notebook.

This approach demonstrates the importance of keeping our data loose. This is why, when I create documentation panels now, I prefer using large foam panels and thumbtacks. This allows me to bring different concepts and questions to the panel, find new affinities, and mix and remix my data for different purposes. Historically, documentation panels have been about telling a single story about a learning experience. When we work the panel and encourage others to put their eyes and hands on it, new and different theories emerge. Some value digital tools for this same potential, and I do, too. There's much to be said about holding these data in our hands, though. Amanda O. Latz asks, "What is the difference between handling a photo and viewing it?" (2017, p. 86). And this is a worthy question. I find that the haptic nature of interactive documentation panels aids us in seeing things we might not, otherwise. The act of physically moving, placing, mixing, and replacing these data adds something to our analyses that scrolling, sorting, and clicking cannot. Your experiences may differ, and if so, I'd love to hear from you.

## Learning Walls

As my work with documentation panels began to deviate from what I'd first encountered in Reggio Emilia schools, I became even more fascinated by Jessica Vance's work. A former IB PYP (International Baccalaureate Primary Years Programme) Educator and PYP (Primary Years Programme) Coordinator, Jess uses learning walls—something she conceived herself—to facilitate deep inquiry work with students and teachers in Texas. I introduced earlier in this text, no chapter on interpreting data would be complete without serious attention to her learning walls concept.

A learning wall begins with an idea, and that idea might be big or small. Those ideas are represented on the wall, and then learners continue to make their thinking and learning visible as they explore, expand, and refine the idea over time. When teachers add to the learning wall, they model inquiry, reflection, and cognitive flexibility for their students. Rather than presenting as a content expert or the proverbial "sage on the stage," teachers who build and work learning walls with their students help them understand that learning is complex and that ideas are highly contextualized and evolving things. Learning walls reflect our curiosities and make the meaning-making process visible to all. When students add their own ideas to the wall, they're better able to trace the influence of their contributions on their peers and their teachers as well. These are the four steps that Jess recommends to those who are getting started with this work:

◆ Build the wall around a meaningful intention and make it clear to everyone in the community. Perhaps you're trying to solve a problem, chasing an essential question, or learning more about a concept. Identify it clearly, and center it in your work.

◆ Think about what you hope to retrieve from learners. Instead of planning to input knowledge, consider the skills you would like them to hone. Make observations and gather evidence of this. Add it to the wall.

◆ Leave room for wonder and curiosity. Invite learners to engage with the wall, co-create meaning from its contents, and pursue knotty questions together. Use the discoveries made during this step to plan your next ones, instructionally. Help them see how they're shaping what happens next.

◆ Rely on the wall as a third teacher. As it evolves, engage learners with it for reflective purposes, coach quality questioning, and use it as a tool that can challenge and even change their thinking.

Finally, know that learning walls are a reflection of current reality. They're messy, meandering, and, often, unsustainable. It's okay to take them down once they've served their purpose. You may choose to keep an artifact or two or none at all. Save what's useful to the next bend in your inquiry work. Let go of what's been processed. Follow Jess on Instagram at jess_vanceedu to explore examples and learn more about her process (jess_vanceedu, 2023).

## Broadening Your Learning Community

The next chapter of this book will further address the social nature of pedagogical documentation, including strategies for building and sustaining a professional learning network inside of different online communities. As the landscape within each is constantly changing in response to the interests and needs of its owners and (sadly, less often, its users), I struggle to recommend any single space with confidence. As I write this, I'm active on LinkedIn, Twitter, and Instagram. I remain connected to the network I trust through multiple channels now, though. If one goes down, I will find them on another. More importantly, our thinking and work together have evolved in such a way that I can reach out through text messages or email now. I can invite the friends I need to put eyes on my documentation efforts in a just-right way at a just-right time. I'm especially sensitive to who might offer the best perspective inside of a specific context, too. This is what I want for you.

When you broaden your learning community, you have the opportunity to mitigate bias if you're intentional about it. You also open up a world of wonder and find your people, too. Before the Internet, so many passionate teachers felt alone in their interests and work. This remains the case today. Too many schools remain plagued by cultures of scarcity that foment fear and stoke bitter rivalries and competition. Teachers who connect to other professionals online often tell me they weather these storms a bit better. Rather than waiting on conferences and other opportunities to leave their systems long enough to find good company, teachers who use social media tools to find like-minded and wholehearted colleagues outside of their systems often sustain their professional learning and contribute to that of others on an almost daily basis.

Documentation plays an important role here. When I scroll through the posts shared inside my own professional learning network, I notice that many serve as powerful examples of pedagogical documentation. The comments that follow reveal impressive levels of analysis as well. And because this is happening in an open space, there's great potential to tap and build collective expertise. Many have built and sustained deep and lasting relationships with one another this way. Their circles are resilient, and they stand the test of time. A certain level of forming, storming, and norming has occurred, and as a result, contributors are able to offer criteria-specific cool feedback, challenge one another's thinking and perspective, and even call each other in when there is potential for decisions or words to do harm.

How we choose to share and invite diverse perspectives online or elsewhere depends on a number of critical factors. Balancing opportunity and risk, protecting our own privacy and our students' as well, and taking care to nurture the commons require intentional and careful decision-making. The next chapter of this book will prepare you to make good choices here before you begin planning your own documentation project using the tools available in Part III.

## TLDR (Too Long, Didn't Read)

1. Analytic memos are one way to begin interpreting our evidence of learning, even as we are still capturing it.
2. Experienced documentarians might borrow practices from grounded theory researchers who document and display their evidence, engage in open, axial, selective, and theoretical coding, as well as memo writing.
3. In order to mitigate bias, it's essential that documentarians seek diverse perspectives as they plan and execute their work. Critical friends are important, too.
4. Documentation panels, notebooks, and learning walls support co-created meaning-making, and there are a variety of ways to use them.

**Let's Reflect**

How might you use documentation panels, documentation notebooks, or learning walls in your own work? Think about this and perhaps jot yourself a note or two about the things you might do.

**Try This: Just Right Tools and Invitations**

Analyze a moment, a journey, or a learning expedition. Practice coding your data, and if you'd like more inspiration and ideas to try, visit the resources and tools in the appendix to learn more.

## References

Goodman, Y., & Owocki, G. (2002). *Kidwatching: Documenting children's literacy development*. Heinemann.

Hattie, J. (2023). *Visible learning: The sequel*. Taylor & Francis.

Kashin, D. (2016, April 26). *The three elements of the documentation process—moving beyond display to interpretation*. Technology Rich Inquiry Based Research. https://tecribresearch.blog/2013/04/02/the-three-elements-of-the-documentation-process-moving-beyond-display-to-interpretation/

Latz, A. O. (2017). *Photovoice research in education and beyond: A practical guide from theory to exhibition*. Routledge, Taylor & Francis Group.

Rinaldi, C. (2021). *In dialogue with Reggio Emilia: Listening, researching, and learning*. Routledge, Taylor & Francis Group.

Stockman, A. (2022). *The writing workshop teacher's guide to multimodal composition: 6-12*. Routledge, Taylor & Francis Group.

Vance, J. [@jess_vanceedu]. (2023, February 12). Four questions that have launched action, playful thinking about our spaces & stretched classroom teachers and leaders around the globe to reconsider the role of the "third teacher" over the past month. [Photographs]. Instagram.https://www.instagram.com/p/CokhP9fORze/?utm_source=ig_web_copy_link&igshid=MzRlODBiNWFlZA==

# 8

# How Will You Seek Diverse Perspectives Along the Way?

I began documenting my own learning in order to better understand the impact that my teaching methods were having on learners. It's helped me understand so much more though, and it's the unexpected lessons that sustain my commitment to this work. Documentation helps me stay above the fray when pedagogical tensions rise up within the field. It keeps me centered on what matters most, and it pushes me to interrogate how I'm defining that for myself or encouraging those I serve to do the same. Documentation makes me an accountable and reflective practitioner. I know that it's not enough to simply lift "best practices" and then drop them into my own classroom. I need to study their fit. I need to understand whether what's best for the masses is truly best for the small group of learners I serve. I need to adapt and adjust until I have evidence to suggest that I'm getting it right. This keeps me engaged. It makes me a passionate practitioner, and while much has been said about the benefits of that reality, the fact is that passion creates bias as well. How should we handle that?

> 🔦 Engagement isn't synonymous with fun, so if you're struggling to document your learning but that struggle is productive, ask yourself what needs to change in order for you to remain committed to your work. You may need to adjust your framing, tools, point of view, or timing in order to make the experience manageable. You may need to pause the project entirely as you confront unexpected challenges, but if this is the case, begin planning to resume the journey or expedition in the future. Often, the most uncomfortable learning we do is also the most important.

DOI: 10.4324/9781003333241-11

## Defining Strengths and Needs

As a young teacher, it was not uncommon for me to sit in rooms where staff developers told me how I might teach best, based on the recommendations of popular researchers in the field and then eventually, standardized assessment results. I would listen and dutifully report back to my classroom, where the problems discussed in those meetings suddenly came into sharp relief. I noticed them more. In fact, it wasn't uncommon for me to begin noticing them to the exclusion of everything—and everyone—else.

Eager to do right by my students and close the gaps illuminated in our professional development sessions, I practiced the strategies offered to me with fidelity. They rarely worked as promised, and this was demoralizing at times. So, I began adapting them in order to meet the needs of the learners I served, and I discovered much along the way. At the time, I thought I was doing it all wrong. I thought I was cheating—breaking the rules. Now, I know that I was practicing beginner-level inquiry work. Over time, this evolved into a practice that looked much like action research, although it would be years before I formalized my approach. I share this here because the most important lesson learned was this: Until we're able to access the voices of the learners we serve and study the impact of a practice on their dispositional growth as well as their performance and the processes they use, our understanding of their strengths and needs is incomplete. Even when learners have a voice in this decision-making process, these stories remain incomplete. Learning and learners are complex, and so is teaching. This is why documentation and diverse perspective-taking matters. The journey never ends. There is always more to learn. There are always better ways to serve.

> ✎ How do you define the strengths and needs of learners you serve? How do you invite them to co-construct entry points into your own documentation work with you? Relying on multiple measures is critical here, and how you go about gathering and interpreting them is consequential.

## Multiple Measures

I'm often asked how we can be sure that the theories we're creating are truly meaningful or even responsible ones. Multiple measures matter. When I use single data points to reach hard and fast conclusions about anyone's strengths or needs, those conclusions lack important nuance. Often, they're entirely incorrect. This is why, whenever I begin to use evidence of any kind to create theories about learners or learning (including my own), I call it what it is: a beginning. Then, I work to define the additional points of data that might better inform, refine, or completely change our perspectives.

When I'm invited to work with data teams in schools, I'm often presented with incomplete standardized assessment findings. Some hope that I'll rush to conclusions here and settle teachers into the work of rapidly improving performance.

When teachers invite me to work with them in different contexts, they often present me with incomplete collections of qualitative data that illuminate fascinating phenomena occurring in their classrooms. Some hope that I'll use this information to advocate for different standards or expectations.

And when I work with children, they often present me with incomplete responses to the questions that I ask or answers that point me down pathways I never intended to travel. Few have any expectations of me. They're simply sharing their experiences and, if I'm fortunate, their thoughts and feelings about them.

All of these data matter.

When I am able to bring multiple measures together, they inform one another and help learners of all kinds shape better questions to pursue. The documentation projects that emerge from this sort of work are typically far more productive and less harmful than other intervention plans might be.

One of the best ways to seek diverse perspectives is to diversify the measures you are using to define the needs and opportunities that you root your documentation projects within. It's important to remember that even as your data work becomes robust, causality is nearly impossible to establish. Our practices remain precisely that—practices. When we take care to contextualize, document, and analyze how they work, those practices improve. When we don't, they often fail to provide a just-right fit for learners, and our expertise isn't strengthened by our work with them either.

If I've learned anything from documentation, it's that teaching is a great experiment, and assessment provides insight—not answers. I may have more or less confidence in some of the things that I discover, but I have to remain humble if I'm going to serve others and my own learning well.

## Co-creating Our Documentation Projects

I've shared examples of co-creative documentation practices throughout this book, but I think it's especially important to offer a deeper treatment here, inside a chapter that speaks to diverse perspective-taking. When we create and execute documentation projects in isolation, our learning and the findings from our work are a reflection of who we are, what we know, our experiences, and how we see the world. When we invite others to collaborate with us throughout the process, this widens our aperture. This allows us to understand and serve different kinds of learners well.

It's important to invite diverse perspectives at different points in the documentation experience, as illustrated in Figure 8.1. Taking care to identify those who might make the best contribution to our work takes a bit of time. Engaging them in just-right ways matters, too. If you're a beginner, committed to documenting a single moment or a handful of them in order to better understand the learners you serve, it makes sense to engage those learners in the process. If you're an experienced documentarian engaged in a sustained learning expedition that involves documenting what you learn about people and the processes they use in different places, you'll want to engage that specific community, but you might also consider drawing on the expertise of those who conceptualized the process, those that will be most impacted by it, and critical friends whose identities and experiences enable them to recognize things that all of you do

## Inviting Diverse Perspectives

When we invite the people we're interested in learning about and from to co-create documentation projects with us and then, capture and interpret evidence of learning, their perspectives have a far greater influence on our own.

When we invite critical friends and even skeptics to share their feedback and their own interpretations of our data, we are made better aware of flaws in our thinking, the potential unintended consequences of our work, and how we might potentially be planning to do harm or worse-- possibly causing it.

When it isn't possible to invite subjects, critical friends, or skeptics to join us in our work, it's important that we remain honest about the potential for bias and other limitations in our findings.

**Before**

**During**

**After**

### Before Documenting

- Co-create the project with those who will be most affected by it.
- Invite critical friends to share their feedback and suggestions.
- Invite those whose identities are different from your own to do the same.

### As You Document

- Invite your subjects to document beside you.
- Invite colleagues to do the same.
- Invite feedback from critical friends and those whose identities are different from your own.

### As You Interpret Data

- Invite your subjects to share their insights first.
- Invite colleagues to do the same.
- Invite critical friends and even-- skeptics--to share their perspectives.
- Invite others to interpret your data in your absence and without the greater context of the project.

*Figure 8.1—Inviting Diverse Perspectives*

not. What if your intention is to better understand a culturally diverse group whose race, gender, ethnicity, or abilities are different from your own? Whose perspectives do you need? When? How might you access them?

## Finding Critical Friends

The best critical friends are those who are able to push and challenge our practices and our thinking. They aren't invested in being right, and they don't set out to prove anyone wrong. Rather, they help us consider things we may not have otherwise—especially the limitations of our perspectives. This is an essential part of doing good documentation work. If you're someone who lives, works, and learns within richly diverse communities, your ability to invite and sustain critical friendships is greater than that of those who travel in more homogeneous circles. So, how do we find critical friends in those circumstances? And how might we proceed when we can't?

Most of my critical friends are educators and other scholars I've become acquainted with through the professional learning network I maintain online. I've been active there for nearly twenty years in one capacity or another, and my engagement with different groups across different networks has helped me meet and build relationships with people I can count on to offer solid feedback on my thinking and work. Building those kinds of relationships is key, but this takes time. It also requires that we give as much as we expect to take and respect our colleague's time and position.

For instance, while my work may benefit from the perspectives of those who live on the margins, my work is not their work, and their labor should be paid for. I also need to recognize that many of the biases I'm striving to mitigate are ones that have done great harm to these same critical friends and the people they care about, too. They may not have the emotional reserves to deal with the reality of that in service to my interests or needs. And finally, depending on the context I intend to share my findings within, certain critical friends may be more or less inclined to contribute to any project.

When I'm unable to include the right critical friends on any project, committing to a robust literature review becomes even more important. When I'm unable to access people and gain their perspectives directly, I search for books, articles, videos, and other professional learning experiences that broaden my knowledge and deepen my awareness of all that I may not yet know. I share this learning with those in my network who are available and eager to help me learn and do better. Most importantly, I keep the limitations of my work in mind, given its design and my access to critical friends—or lack thereof. And I'm honest about those limitations when I share findings from my work.

## Social Sharing

It can also make sense to leverage your social networks in service to better learning and documentation work. Ensuring that your students' privacy is protected and that you've considered the unintended consequences of such choices is an important first step, but whenever we share images, videos, or reflections of any kind on social media, we're essentially making our documentation work visible to others and inviting their commentary. Becoming far more intentional about what we share, where, and why often elevates the way we engage as well as the rewards of those efforts. Social sharing is one way to lightly engage critical friends, and sometimes those initial exchanges can grow into deeper learning opportunities—especially if we've been thoughtful about who we follow and engage in those spaces.

*Klara is committed to decolonizing her curriculum and her practices as well. It's no surprise then that, as our conversations about teaching and learning have evolved, so too have her thoughts about Indigenous ways of knowing and how biased our understanding of pedagogical documentation might be. I lack understanding here. I'm eager to deepen my own awareness, too. As we learned in a previous chapter, Klara continues to learn and often—relearn Indigenous histories and how Indigenous world views and learning models can help us build a community of documentarians through a different lens.*

*Social sharing is advantageous in this way, too: When we share what we're learning, others identify with our interests and often reach out with similar needs. And when we position ourselves as learners rather than experts in social spaces, those within our network feel comfortable revealing this and assuming the postures of critical friends. When they have expertise we need, and when we take care to maintain our connections to them and reciprocate in kind, we begin to reap the rewards of connected, social learning. They're far greater than mere networking provides. In my experience, these are the highest purposes of social networks. These are the greatest gifts of being a connected educator.*

## Publication

Publication is another way of getting good eyes and minds on your documentation work. Too often, educators publish in order to share their expertise.

I do the same, but each book that I've published is the result of a documentation project, I am careful to assert this, and I position myself as a learner seeking feedback and garnering the interest of those who would like to test the ideas I'm sharing and then, report back with their findings and engage critical friends of their own. Sometimes, I'm directly involved in this experience. Other times, I'm able to observe and learn from the wings. Regardless, I find that publication is often the best way to widely test my theories and have my documentation approaches and assumptions challenged. Publication inspires validation and criticism. It consistently refines my thinking and the way that I teach and facilitate professional learning, too.

I'm not suggesting that you need to write a book. You might begin blogging, start a Substack or newsletter, present at a conference, or submit an article to an education journal. I'm not suggesting that you have to have certainty about the ideas that you share within your work, either. Just be honest about this. Explain that your ideas are highly experimental, that you're still in the midst of learning, and that the ideas you are sharing in this place and time are a reflection of your current learning, which is still very much in process. It's refreshing when I encounter pieces like these, and as I'm writing this, I wonder how many tensions might have been mitigated within the current literacy landscape had experts been less certain, prescriptive, and, at times, even judgmental about the right or wrong way to do engage in certain processes or practices. I'm reminded all over again of Jess Vance's wisdom. Leave room for curiosity, she tells us. Leave room for our evolution too, I might add.

If you choose to publish your ideas for the purposes I describe here, you'll want to invite your readers to connect with and challenge you. Offer them a vehicle for doing so, and share approaches or even protocols that ensure a productive exchange if you feel that's necessary. You'll find examples in my digital documentation notebook.

*You might invite your students or other visitors to publish about your work with your consent. I've learned so much about how my ideas are interpreted and what's most resonant about my documentation efforts this way. For instance, I was recently invited to facilitate a pop-up studio event for middle and high school writers in Cuba, New York. A hundred or more learners showed up to explore and experiment with multimodal composition over the course of a full school day, and I relished the opportunity to document my learning. You'll find some of that work beside my reflections from that day in my digital documentation notebook, and I hope they are useful to you.*

*For the first time ever, I had the opportunity to engage a documentary maker in this same work, though. Silence Karl, the videographer whose reflections were shared in Chapters 1 and 4 of this book, was tasked with capturing our learning stories that day. Event leaders were eager to document the energy in the room, participants' learning stories, and my own perspectives on this work in order to build regional awareness of the kinds of professional and student-learning experiences they were bringing to area schools. You'll find the video he created about this experience in my digital documentation notebook. I intentionally offered no guidance about what was most meaningful to capture that day, and so viewing it helps me understand what this outside observer felt was most important about the work and what it meant to learners in the room. It was eye-opening, and I'm eager to replicate this project in other contexts soon. I wonder: How might you do something similar, in order to glimpse an outside observer's interpretation of your work? What would the benefits be?*

## Aligning Our Purposes and Practices

As you've moved through each chapter of this book, you've learned more about what documentation is, how you might approach it, and how your purposes and practices might shift as you gain experience. I've been deliberate about distinguishing beginner-level work from that of practiced documentarians, and this is because, in my experience, when documentarians take on more than they might be ready for, they abandon the process entirely. As you prepare to use the third part of this book to plan your own documentation project, I wonder: What will your purposes be? Now might be a good time to revisit the Documentation Kaleidoscope, skim through the notes you've made as you've wove your way through this text, and dig into my digital documentation notebook again. Which ideas and examples move you? What would you like to try?

Once you're become clear about your purposes, you'll be ready to make more deliberate decisions about seeking diverse perspectives, too. For instance, it may not be necessary or realistic for you to publish your work for the world to see. You may not have the funds to pay critical friends to review your work. Perhaps you simply want to document a moment in order to remember it. Do you need to call critical friends to the analysis table then? Perhaps not, but what might you discover if you were able to?

Here are the things that I consider each time I think about seeking diverse perspectives:

◆ I wonder who will be most impacted by my documentation work and how having different perspectives might ensure that there is no harm done.

◆ I wonder about the complexity of what I'm trying to capture. What will be easy for me to observe? What will escape my notice entirely? What might be the consequences of this reality?

◆ How might I make my students co-collaborators in my planning and documentation work as it unfolds?

◆ How might I bring my local colleagues into this work?

◆ When or where would it make sense to engage more distant, critical friends? How might I do this? And what if I can't find them? What could I read, listen to, or view that might inform or change my perspective?

◆ And how might publishing my project in whole or in part invite a wider and more informed process? How could I do that? Where? Why would I?

If you're a beginner, it makes sense to co-create documentation projects that aim to better understand students with the students you intend to serve better. This might look like sharing your intentions with them, conducting a needs and interests assessment, inviting them to make learning visible, and then, once you've displayed your documentation, invite them to share their interpretations of that evidence and co-construct theories about it with you. These theories will inform your next steps as a learning community, a teacher, and a documentarian. These efforts will remain highly experimental. You might also connect them to other inquiry work.

As you gain experience and confidence in the theories you're testing together, you might begin to share them with a wider audience. You may blog about them or share your findings and reflections inside a social media update in order to garner a wider audience and new perspectives about your work. You may expand that audience further by presenting at a conference, contributing to a poster session, or submitting an article to an education journal.

At some point, your theories will likely become promising practices that appear to have a consistently positive effect on learners and learning, you might consider more serious publication options. Contrary to what many believe, it isn't as difficult to find a home for a new book these days. That's problematic, too. Not every publisher applies the same critical lens to the proposals they receive or the manuscripts they accept. Some care more about sales than they do about the impact of the theories these books espouse. As you consider publication, take care to define your own boundaries here. Investigate the houses you intend to approach, reach out to some of their authors to solicit their feedback and experiences, and ask a lot of questions along the way. Your editors will offer additional points of view for you to consider. As you do, ask whose voices may still be missing. Ask yourself how you might access them. Then, do that. It matters.

## TLDR (Too Long, Didn't Read)

1. Responsible documentarians rely on multiple measures of evidence as they create theories about learners and learning.
2. When we co-create documentation projects with those who will be most impacted by their results, this helps to mitigate bias—especially when we invite those same people to interpret the findings with us.
3. When we struggle to find the right critical friends for a project, it's even more important to turn to the literature of the field and find the right expert voices and different perspectives in order to inform our work.
4. The professional learning networks we build and sustain online include many who might serve as great critical friends. If we take care to engage them in ways that protect everyone's privacy and respect the consents given.
5. We might also publish with the intention to seek diverse perspectives.

## Let's Reflect

How might you ensure that your process is a richly social one that pulls on the perspectives of the people you intend to serve as well as critical friends? How might you mitigate bias when achieving this isn't possible?

## Try This: Just Right Tools and Invitations

◆ Co-create a documentation project with the people you intend to serve. Document a moment together in order to practice coding the data.
◆ Or, document a journey together while making intentional use of multiple measures.
◆ Or, engage a group of critical friends in meaning-making by sharing the evidence gathered over the course of a lengthy learning expedition.

# Part III

# Tools and Resources

# Digital Documentation Notebook

Dear Readers,

Throughout this text, I've made continual reference to my digital documentation notebook. Here, you will find clear examples of the approaches I speak to, case and use studies that demonstrate their use, and contributions from other documentarians I admire in the field.

Please access my notebook on my website (https://angelastockman.com/blog/2023/08/02/my-digital-documentation-notebook/) using the password Documentarian. This is a living document that can evolve over time in response to your interests and needs, so please contact me (https://angelastockman.com/contact/) if you'd like to share either or both. I'm looking forward to learning from you.

Warm regards,
Angela

DOI: 10.4324/9781003333241-13

# Planning a Documentation Project

Dear Readers,

This is an assessment that can help you begin to:

- ◆ Define a greater vision for your work before thinking about project-specific purposes;
- ◆ Consider whether your documentation approach will test an existing idea or theory or help you uncover and create new ones;
- ◆ Identify what you might document when and for how long.

What follows are a series of questions that will challenge you to reflect and then make some choices. You may find it useful to write your responses in a notebook or a journal. You might choose to write your responses in a digital document or audio or video record your reflections instead.

Please know that there are no right or wrong answers here. In fact, you may wander away from some of these questions uncertain about your responses, and that's okay.

You may return to this assessment anytime in order to refine or even completely revise your plan. This tool is less about helping you make hard and fast decisions and more about helping you establish habits and thinking routines that make planning to document your learning meaningful and manageable.

DOI: 10.4324/9781003333241-14

I hope you find this process useful, and your feedback is welcome! Please email me at stockmanangela@gmail.com if you'd like to share your perspectives.

Thank you,
Angela

## Consider Your Greater Vision

What do you hope to achieve by becoming a teacher who documents their learning? Rather than thinking about a specific project that unfolds in a specific place during a specific period of time for a specific purpose, consider this:

*If you were to document your own learning for the remainder of your career, how do you hope it will serve you? How do you hope it will change you and your relationship with teaching for the better?*

If you'd like to spend some additional time constructing a meaningful vision for your documentation work, these invitations (bit.ly/3sFJ34M) might be useful to you.

## Align Your Purposes with Your Vision

Now that you're becoming more aware of your greater vision for documenting your learning over time, think about ONE specific project you'd like to begin in the near future. What are the purposes for this?

Why will you do it, and what do you hope to learn in the process? How do these distinct purposes—for one very specific project—align with and support your greater vision?

*Will you document to simply REMEMBER someone or something? If so, go to section 2.*

*Will you document in order to better UNDERSTAND someone or something? If so, go to section 3.*

*Or, will you document in order to SERVE someone or something better? If so, go to section 4.*

## Section 2: Documenting to Remember Someone or Something That Mattered

Documentarians capture what they see and hear within a moment or a series of moments. This engages them in their learning, makes them more present and aware, and leaves them with lasting artifacts that they can return to after the experience is over in order to remember it.

The following series of questions will help you REMEMBER someone or something that mattered.

When we test established ideas and theories, our process is deductive. When we document in order to create ideas and theories, our process is inductive. Our intentions here influence our planning.

If you aren't quite certain about your purposes and your plan is still feeling a bit nebulous, an inductive process might help you find a meaningful path forward.

*Will your project aim to test ideas or theories that you or someone else has already established? Go to section 5 to plan a deductive process.*

*Will you use what you learn from documenting your learning to establish ideas and theories instead? Go to section 6 to plan an inductive process.*

## Section 3: Documenting in Order to Serve

When we document to serve someone or something better, we take care to capture our observations about people, places, processes, practices, or products. Which of these will you document in order to study and better understand them?

The following series of questions will enable you to SERVE yourself or others better.

When we test established ideas and theories, our process is deductive. When we document in order to create ideas and theories, our process is inductive. Our intentions here influence our planning.

If you aren't quite certain about your purposes and your plan is still feeling a bit nebulous, an inductive process might help you find a meaningful path forward.

*Will your project aim to test ideas or theories that you or someone else has already established? Go to section 5.*

*Will you use what you learn from documenting your learning to establish ideas and theories instead? Go to section 6.*

## Section 4: Documenting to Understand

Documentarians capture what they see and hear within a moment or a series of moments. This engages them in their learning, makes them more present and aware, and leaves them with lasting artifacts that they can return to after the experience is over in order to analyze what occurred and what it may have meant. This is a powerful way to better understand ourselves, others, our experiences, and the effects of the decisions we make.

The following series of questions will help you seek understanding as a documentarian.

When we test established ideas and theories, our process is deductive. When we document in order to create ideas and theories, our process is inductive. Our intentions here influence our planning.

If you aren't quite certain about your purposes and your plan is still feeling a bit nebulous, an inductive process might help you find a meaningful path forward.

*Will your project aim to test ideas or theories that you or someone else has already established? Go to section 5.*

*Will you use what you learn from documenting your learning to establish ideas and theories instead? Go to section 6.*

## Section 5: Making a Deductive Study to Test Preexisting Ideas or Theories

The questions that follow can help you plan to test ideas, theories, and best practices in your own learning context. In order to ensure a deductive process, you will need to define what those ideas, theories, and practices are first. Which of them would you like to study? And how will you do this?

Before you continue, pause right here for a moment and think about how you might create an experience that will enable this well. You may want to sketch something up or make a few notes. The prompts that follow will help you refine that plan and make space for documentation.

If your documentation project is deductive, you will consider the impact of an idea, theory, or practice on learning or learners.

Many find themselves documenting different aspects of an experience by studying some combination of the elements below.

Try to use this tool to deepen your awareness of your interests and needs as a documentarian by playing with it. You can revisit this assessment as often as you need, experiment with the different options, and explore varied paths.

Dip into Chapter 5 to explore all of the elements below in greater depth, and use what you learn to clarify your intentions and tighten your plans if things are feeling rather complex and nebulous right now.

*If you plan to document people, go to section 7.*

*If you plan to document places, go to section 8.*

*If you plan to document processes, go to section 9.*

*If you plan to document practices, go to section 10.*

*If you plan to document products, go to section 11.*

## Section 6: Making an Inductive Study to Discover New Ideas and Emerging Theories

If your documentation project is inductive, you will study your learning in order to uncover or discover new ideas or theories rather than testing those that others have developed. What will you investigate?

Note: Many find themselves documenting different aspects of a learning moment by exploring some combination of the elements below. Try to use this tool to deepen your awareness of your interests and needs as a documentarian by playing with it. Dip into Chapter 5 to explore all of the elements below in greater depth, and use what you learn to clarify your intentions and tighten your plans if things are feeling rather complex and nebulous right now.

*If you plan to document people, go to section 16.*

*If you plan to document places, go to section 17.*

*If you plan to document processes, go to section 18.*

*If you plan to document practices, go to section 19.*

*If you plan to document products, go to section 20.*

## Section 7: Making a Deductive Study of People

When you make a deductive study of people, you enter each moment with a predetermined idea, theory, or practice that you're eager to test. Which of these might you bring to your work?

*Now consider the following options. Which of them might help you learn what you intend to do from your project? Go to section 12 when you're ready to move on.*

◆ Study an idea, theory, or practice intended to nurture people's identities, their interests, the funds of knowledge they bring into your community, and their social and emotional strengths and needs.
◆ Study an idea, theory, or practice that attends to people's wishes and their worries, aspirations, goals, and plans.
◆ Study an idea, theory, or practice that might enable them to improve performance as they pursue standards, outcomes, and objectives set for them and those they've set for themselves.
◆ Study an idea, theory, or practice that inspires people to generate and share their interpretations of events that you've both experienced, including learning as you've documented it separately and together.
◆ Study an idea, theory, or practice that helps you determine what learners come to you already able to do or achieve, their attitudes, frames of mind, or tendencies as learners, and the thrill they gain from the learning experience.

*When you're ready, go to section 12.*

## Section 8: Making a Deductive Study of Places

When you make a deductive study of place, you enter it with preconceived ideas, theories, or practices that you intend to test. Which of these might serve you well in your work?

◆ Note the features of the physical environment.
◆ Study how virtual learning spaces are organized. Document what you see and hear relevant to ease of navigation and accessibility.

Capture evidence of how the environment shapes the way that learners engage with content, instructors, and one another, too.

◆ Take note of the cultural environment, gathering evidence of the norms, values, beliefs, and expectations that shape teaching and learning experiences.

◆ Look and listen for evidence of psychological or emotional supports and stressors within the environment.

*When you're ready, go to section 12.*

## Section 9: Making a Deductive Study of Processes

When you make a deductive study of a process, you test preconceived ideas, theories, or practices. Which of these ideas might be useful to try?

◆ Cognitive processes: The mental processes used to perceive, attend to, absorb, and integrate new information. For instance, problem-solving is a cognitive process.

◆ Creative processes as they unfold. As learners engage in inquiry work, design and make things, or engage in the written writing process, documentation helps me notice and take note of the unique ways they approach their work, what works, and what does not.

◆ The things that motivate and demotivate learners. As I explained previously, my first book, *Make Writing* (2015), was my effort to invite diverse perspectives around what I was noticing about writers who initially presented as resistant in my workshops and studios and how unexpected practices, processes, and the environment we created together seemed to be motivating them.

◆ Metacognitive processes: A learner's awareness and understanding of their own process or—as some describe it—their thinking about their thinking.

◆ Concept acquisition: When and how learners relate concepts to one another and deepen their understanding of them, and how they transfer the concepts attained in one context to another one that's entirely new.

*When you're ready, go to section 12.*

## Section 10: Making a Deductive Study of Practices

When you make a deductive study of a practice, you bring preconceived ideas and theories into the work, creating an investigation
that teaches you more about how that idea or theory works in a
given context. Which of these ideas inspire you?

◆ Idea generation practices
◆ Drafting practices
◆ Peer review practices
◆ Revision practices
◆ Editing practices
◆ Specific craft moves

*When you're ready, go to section 12.*

## Section 11: Making a Deductive Study of Products

When we make a deductive study of products, we use preconceived
ideas, theories, or practices to investigate them. Consider each of the
challenges below. Which ideas, theories, or practices might help you
document your learning in this way?

Gather evidence of mastery of knowledge or skills from the products
of learning.

Document growth by capturing products of learning at different
points in time or as learners evolve from apprenticeship to mastery.

Capture shifts in design thinking, process, and craft by studying how
products evolve as well.

Document how learners communicate individually and collaborate
together by creating sociograms.

Invite reflection before a learning experience begins, during the process,
and after the experience has ended. Document what you see and hear.

*When you're ready, go to section 12.*

## Section 12: Consider Your Time Commitment

How much time are you able to commit to this documentation project?

◆ I will document a moment: Something that happens in just one place
at just one time.

- ◆ I will document a journey or a collection of moments.
- ◆ I will document an expedition that unfolds over a series of weeks, months, or even years.

*Go to* section *13 when you're ready.*

## Section 13: Co-Creating Your Project with Those Who Will Be Most Affected by It

When we co-create our documentation plans with those we intend to learn from, those plans tend to serve all of us better. Consider the ideas below as you plan your own documentation project.

I may document a moment to simply remember it. I could ask those I intend to learn from to help me determine which moments are most worth remembering. I could also invite them to simply document for the same purpose—to remember the moment—and compare what they choose to capture to my own documentation work in order to glean their perspectives about what matters.

I may document to better understand someone or something. I could make these intentions clear to those I intend to learn from. Then, I could invite them to "help me understand" their thinking, learning, and/or work before, during, and after the learning moment.

I may document in order to serve others better. I could make those people the subjects of my study and invite their feedback as it unfolds by asking, "What did I do that was helpful to you here?" and "How might I help you better next time?"

*Go to section 14 when you're ready.*

## Section 14: Seeking Diverse Perspectives and Critical Friends

Inviting others to offer their insights and provide feedback on your plans and your documentation project as it unfolds from inception to data interpretation will help you notice things you may not have otherwise and mitigate bias as well. Which of the following approaches will you consider?

- ◆ I will consider whose voices are missing in my planning and my work, and I will invite (but not expect) them to co-plan with me and offer their insights.

◆ I will consider how my identity, positionality, and power might influence the way that I plan and execute my documentation project as well as the interpretations that I make of the findings. I will invite (but not expect) those who are different from me to share their insights.

◆ I will immerse myself in the culture of those I hope to learn more about and from, distinguishing their culture from my own. I will consider the influence of our unique cultural backgrounds on the way we might document and interpret our learning about and in service to one another.

◆ I will read, watch, and listen to texts that help me better understand the perspectives of those who might be very different from me— especially those I intend to learn about and from through my documentation work.

◆ I will establish a professional learning network if I do not yet have one and take care to follow and listen to those whose identities and perspectives are different from my own there.

◆ I will invite those in my professional learning network to offer their insights and feedback on my planning and work.

◆ I will share my plans and work within a wide, diverse network and invite feedback there.

*Go to* section *15 when you're ready.*

## Section 15: Considering Unintended Consequences and Potential Opportunities

Hopefully, this self-assessment has helped you begin to define a vision, purpose, and working plan for your documentation project.

Think a bit about why you plan to document your learning.

Think a bit about how.

Consider your intentions, but then take some time to consider the unintended consequences of the choices you are making. This can help you mitigate bias and harm.

Questions like these are useful.

◆ Who do you intend to serve with your project? Who else might be impacted, though? And how?

◆ How might your work privilege some but not others?

- ◆ Who or what do you intend to learn more about? What else might be revealed along the way?
- ◆ Which questions will guide your inquiry? Are there some you shouldn't pursue? We're never certain of the answers that might be revealed when we start chasing questions. How can you prepare yourself for the unexpected?
- ◆ Documentation projects often lead to the development of ideas and theories that others appreciate and iterate upon. Many make our work their own. What are potential consequences of this? How might you prepare yourself to be responsive?
- ◆ How might your work deepen your relationship with others and strengthen trust? In what ways might it compromise both if you aren't thoughtful in your planning and process?
- ◆ How will documentation change your learning culture and environment? What will be gained? What might be lost? How might you prepare for this?
- ◆ What are the potentially negative unintended consequences of your documentation project? Are they able to be dealt with well, so that harm is not done and your project is not disrupted? If they are not, how will you change your plans or shift your process in order to avoid these consequences entirely? You may have to abandon it entirely. If that's the case, you can use this same assessment and the book itself to start again. Start over. Think and plan differently, this time.

*Go to* section *21 when you're ready.*

## Section 16: Making an Inductive Study of People

When you make an inductive study of people, you maintain a curious and accepting posture. You watch and listen, and you document what you see and hear, without making any judgments or assumptions. Consider these options for your work. Which of them might help you learn what you intend to do from your project?

- ◆ Document what you see and hear about people's identities, their interests, the funds of knowledge they bring into your community, and their social and emotional strengths and needs.
- ◆ Notice and note their wishes, worries, aspirations, goals, and plans.
- ◆ Document their performance as they pursue standards, outcomes, and objectives set for them and those they've set for themselves.

◆ Document their interpretations of events that you've both experienced, including learning as you've documented it separately and together.

◆ Document what learners come to you already able to do or achieve, their attitudes, frames of mind, or tendencies as learners, and the thrill they gain from the learning experience.

*Go to section 12 when you're ready.*

## Section 17: Making an Inductive Study of Places

When you make an inductive study of place, you try to enter it without assumption. You watch and listen, and you document what you see and hear, without imposing or drawing any conclusions. Explore these focal points. Which of them might help you learn what you're hoping to learn from your documentation project?

◆ Note the features of the physical environment.

◆ Study how virtual learning spaces are organized. Document what you see and hear relevant to ease of navigation and accessibility. Capture evidence of how the environment shapes the way that learners engage with content, instructors, and one another, too.

◆ Take note of the cultural environment, gathering evidence of the norms, values, beliefs, and expectations that shape teaching and learning experiences.

◆ Look and listen for evidence of psychological or emotional supports and stressors within the environment.

*Go to section 12 when you're ready.*

## Section 18: Making an Inductive Study of Processes

When you make an inductive study of a process, you capture what you see and hear without bringing any assumptions to the work or making judgments as you gather your data. Consider each of the options below. Which of them might help you learn what you hope to do as a documentarian?

◆ Document cognitive processes at work. These are the mental processes used to perceive, attend to, absorb, and integrate new information. For instance, problem-solving is a cognitive process.

- ◆ Gather evidence of creative processes as they unfold as well. As learners engage in inquiry work, design and make things, or engage in the written writing process, documentation helps me notice and take note of the unique ways they approach their work, what works, and what does not.
- ◆ Pay attention to what motivates and demotivates learners. As I explained previously, my first book, *Make Writing* (2015), was my effort to invite diverse perspectives around what I was noticing about writers who initially presented as resistant in my workshops and studios and how unexpected practices, processes, and the environment we created together seemed to be motivating them.
- ◆ Document metacognitive processes as well. This refers to a learner's awareness and understanding of their own process or—as some describe it—their thinking about their thinking.
- ◆ Document evidence of concept acquisition, when and how learners relate concepts to one another and deepen their understanding of them, and how they transfer the concepts attained in one context to another one that's entirely new.

*When you're ready, go to section 12.*

## Section 19: Making an Inductive Study of Practices

When you make an inductive study of a practice, you capture your observations—what you see and hear—without making an interpretation of them until much later. Consider each of the ideas below as you plan to document your learning about a practice. Which of them might help you uncover something meaningful?

- ◆ Pay attention to the idea generation practices that learners use, and then the way they develop their ideas, capturing evidence along the way.
- ◆ Document the practices learners use to prototype or draft.
- ◆ Take note of how they practice peer review or give and receive feedback.
- ◆ Document evidence of revision, editing, and how learners distinguish them from one another.
- ◆ Make note of the way that writers practice specific craft moves, for effect.

◆ Document the practices that designers use when they assume these different postures: Need finding, problem defining, research, prototyping, testing, and launching.

*When you're ready, go to section 12.*

## Section 20: Making an Inductive Study of Products

When we make an inductive study of products, we suspend judgment while capturing what we see and hear. Consider each of the lenses below. Which of them, when applied to your own project, might help you notice what's most meaningful?

◆ Gather evidence of mastery of knowledge or skills from the products of learning.
◆ Document growth by capturing products of learning at different points in time or as learners evolve from apprenticeship to mastery.
◆ Capture shifts in design thinking, process, and craft by studying how products evolve as well.
◆ Document how learners communicate individually and collaborate together by creating sociograms.
◆ Invite reflection before a learning experience begins, during the process, and after the experience has ended. Document what you see and hear.

*When you're ready, go to section 12.*

## Section 21: Your Feedback Is Welcome

I hope this tool was useful to you, and I'd love your feedback if you're willing to share it. Please drop me a line at stockmanangela@gmail.com if you have insights that might help me improve this work.

Thank you,
Angela

# VISION
## WHAT WILL YOUR LEGACY BE?

I remember the first time anyone asked me this question. My learning community was on retreat, bellies full from our first breakfast together in a year, and hearts hopeful that the week ahead would find us renewed and invigorated again.

"What will your legacy be?" Giselle Martin Kniep asked us, and the room fell silent. We were accustomed to such questions from her—in fact we counted on them—but I have to admit, I felt a little foolish in that moment. I'd never thought of my legacy before. I'm a goal-oriented person, a strategic planner, and an alignment lover at heart. Ask me what my objectives or outcomes may have been for the last 15 years, and I can provide you slides and spreadsheets and bullet journal entries that detail every personal and professional goal I've established and met (or failed to).

What will my LEGACY be, though?

Yeah, I'd never thought of that much until Giselle asked.

And when she asked, that changed everything for me. So, I'm putting the same question in front of you now: What will your legacy be?

*Our legacy is what we leave behind. It's our imprint on this world. It's the difference we make. It's a bit about what we secure for ourselves, but more importantly, it's about what we leave behind, in service to those who will follow us.*

DOI: 10.4324/9781003333241-15

# REFLECT:

I'm at my best as an educator when ...

I'm at my worst as an educator when ...

These are the ways in which my personal self and my educator self get along well ...

These are the ways in which my personal self and educator self are at odds with one another ...

Inside the classroom, I'm especially good at ...

And outside of the classroom, I'm often complimented for ...

The most important thing I would like to understand about my personal self is ...

The most important thing I would like to understand about my educator self is ...

These are the questions eternally engaging me, personally ...

These are my enduring questions as an educator ...

This is the learning that might sustain me over the course of my career or even, my lifetime ...

This is the legacy I hope to leave behind ...

# NOW, CONSTRUCT A VISION:

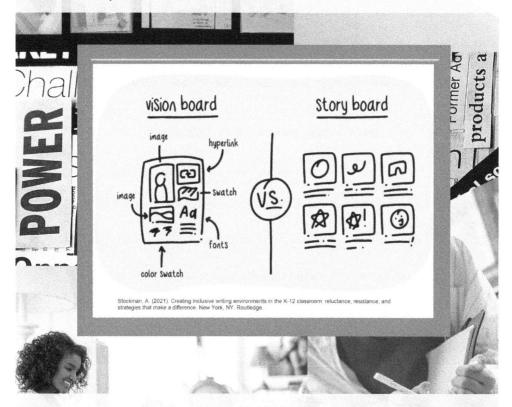

Stockman, A. (2021). Creating inclusive writing environments in the K-12 classroom: reluctance, resistance, and strategies that make a difference. New York, NY: Routledge.

## Consider creating a vision or story board for this.

# Documentation Kaleidoscope

## The Documentation Kaleidoscope

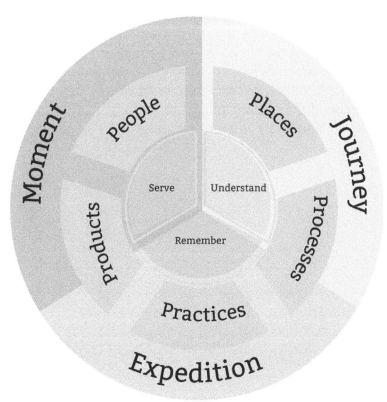

DOI: 10.4324/9781003333241-16

# Recommended Resources

- The National School Reform Faculty Protocols (https://nsrfharmony.org)
- Harvard's Thinking Routine Toolbox (https://pz.harvard.edu/thinking-routines)
- Delve: The Essential Guide to Coding Qualitative Data (https://delvetool.com/guide)
- Dave Gray's Visual Alphabet (https://medium.com/@davegray/in-defense-of-the-visual-alphabet-a8dcca7cf151)
- Gamestorming (https://gamestorming.com)

DOI: 10.4324/9781003333241-17

For Product Safety Concerns and Information please contact our EU
representative  GPSR@taylorandfrancis.com
Taylor & Francis Verlag GmbH, Kaufingerstraße 24, 80331 München, Germany